Leaf

DAISHU
MA

DAISHU
MA

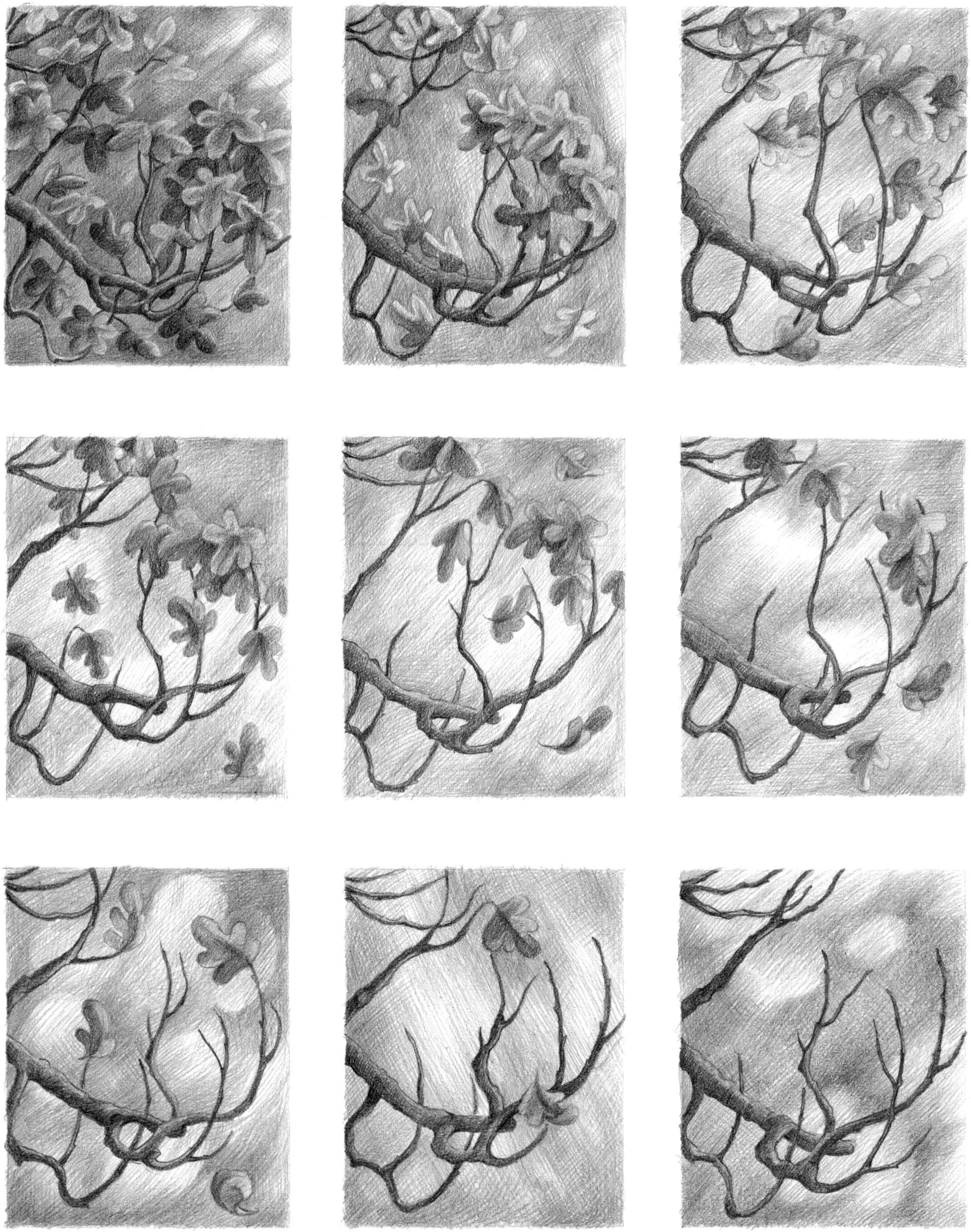

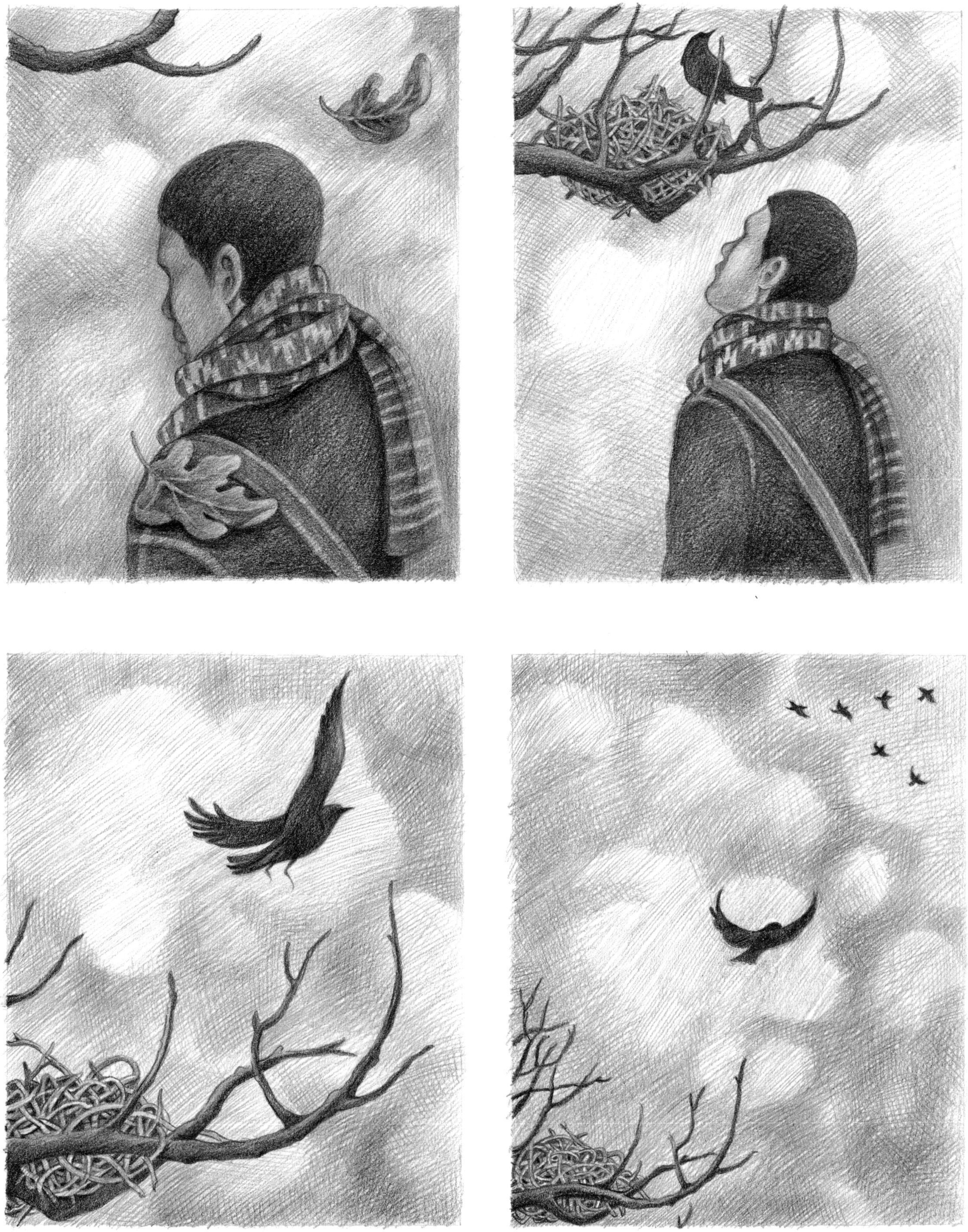

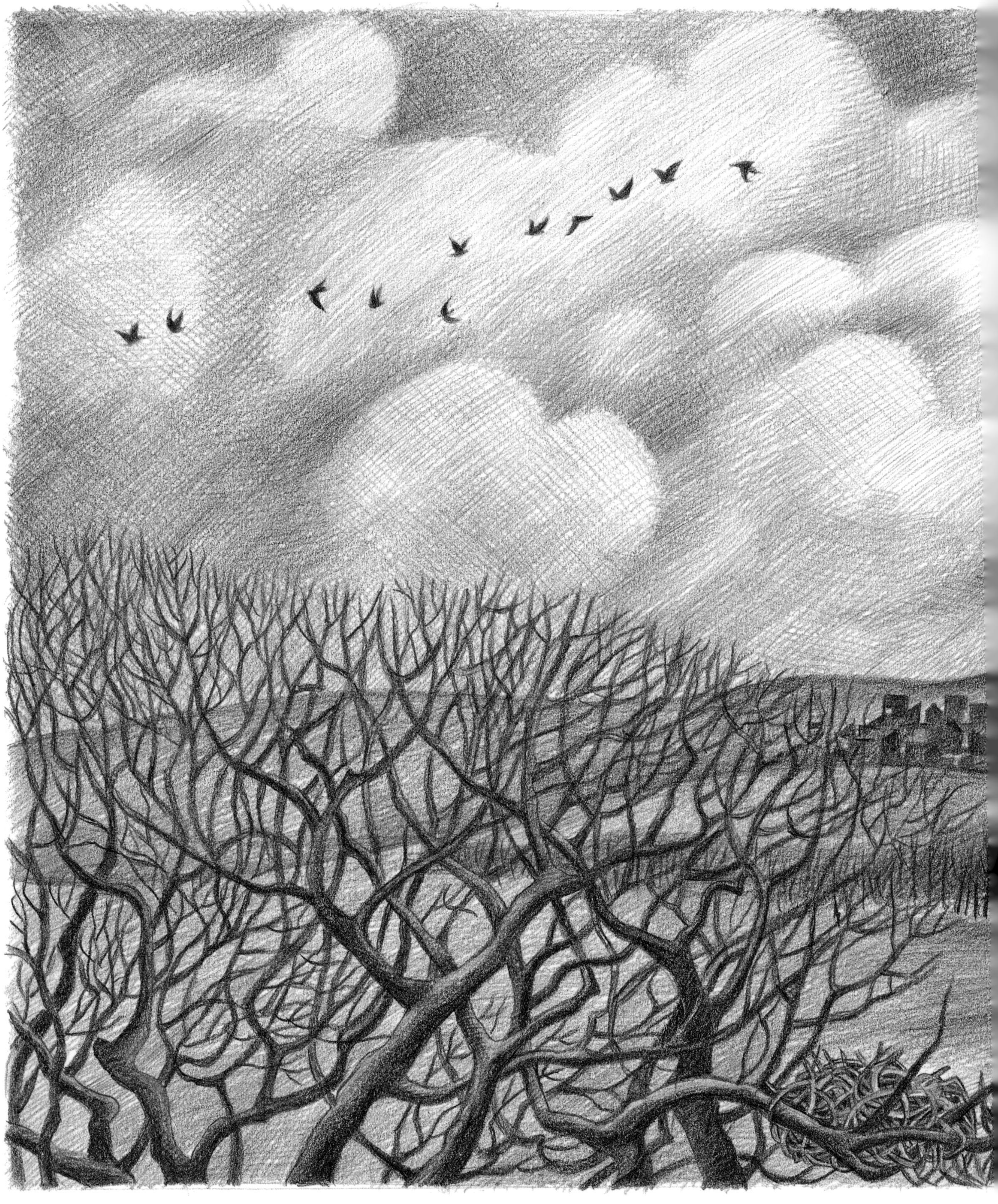

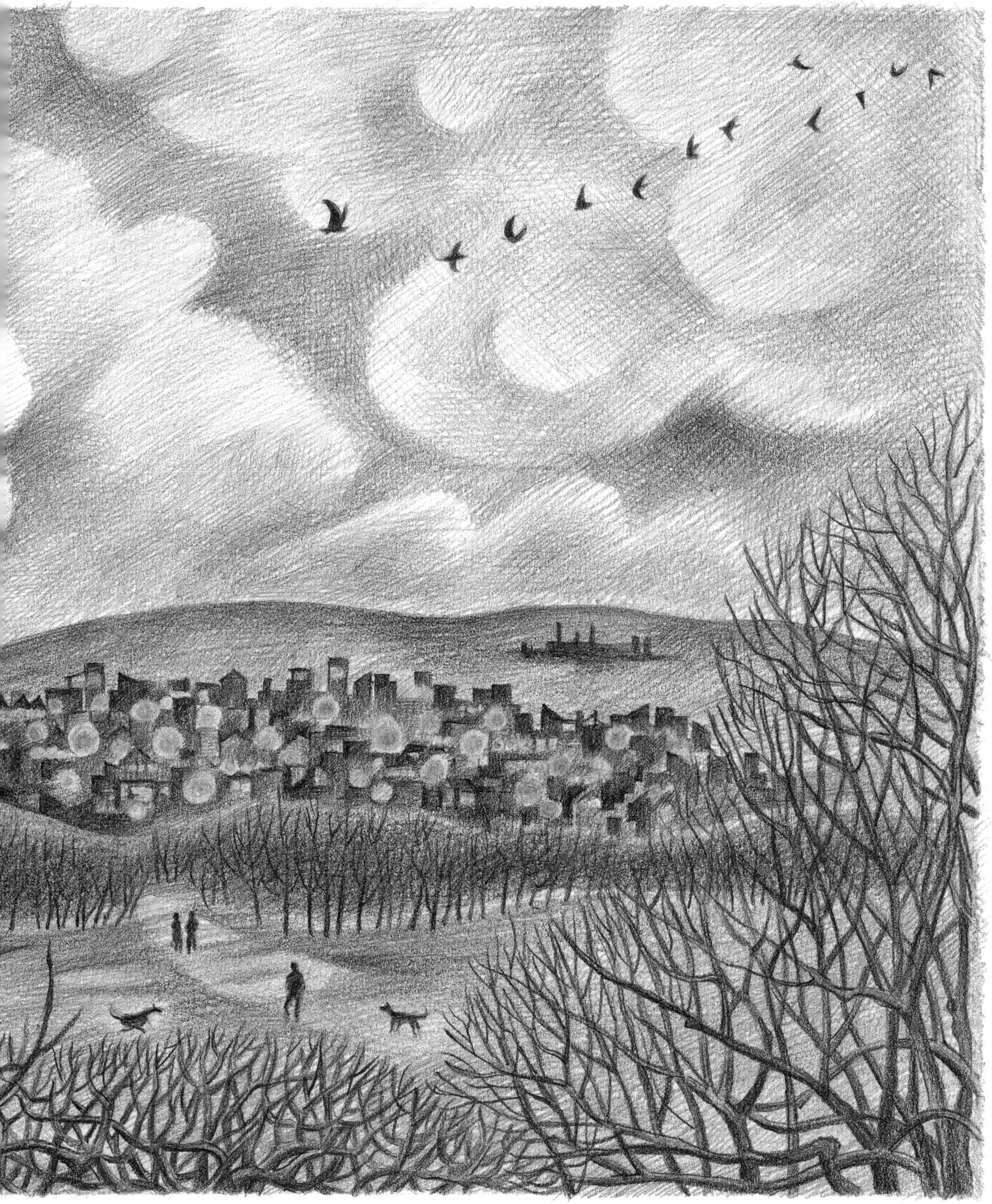

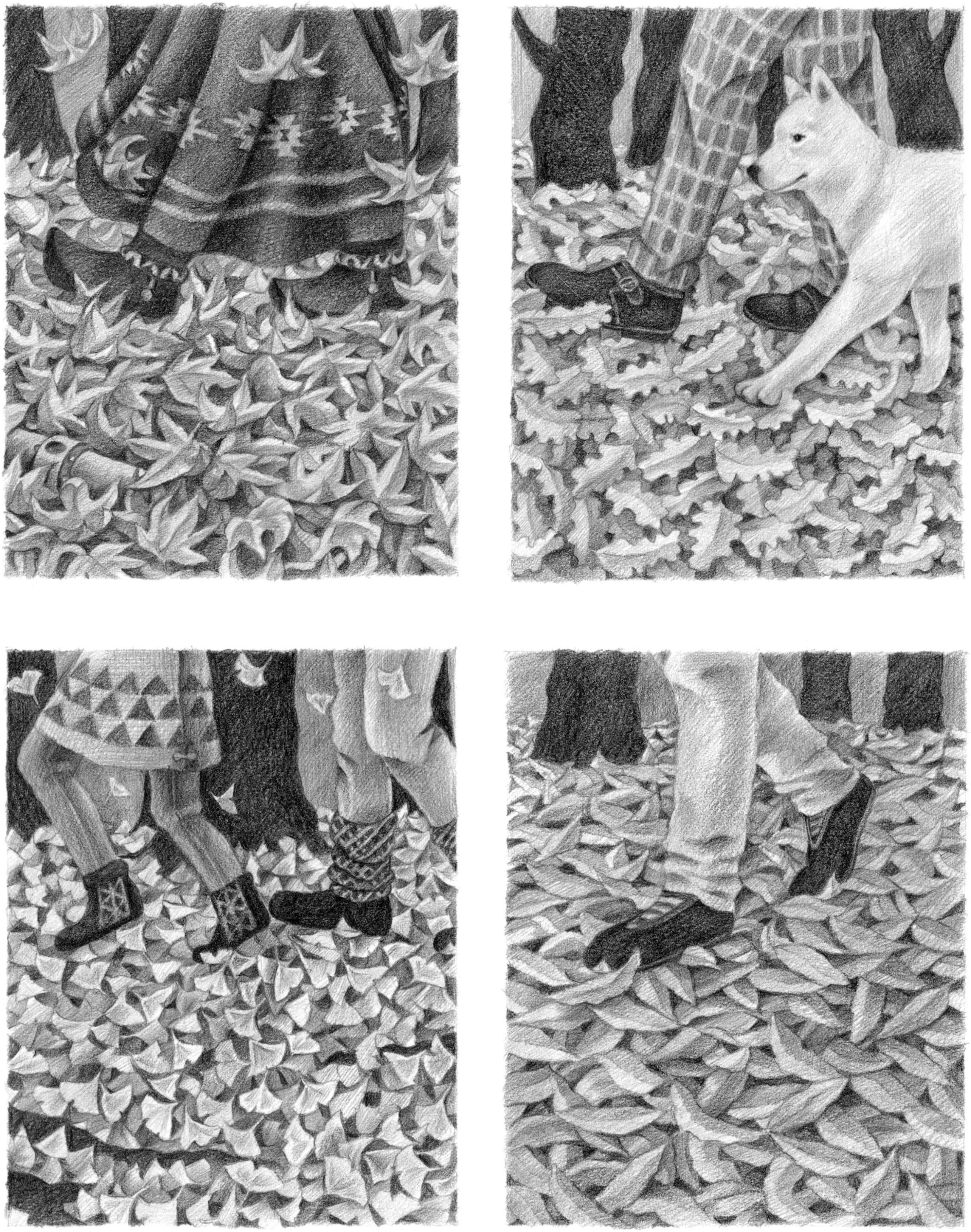

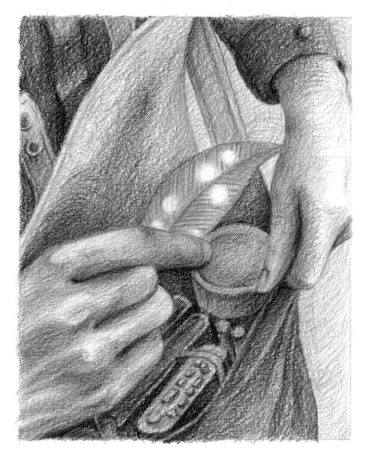

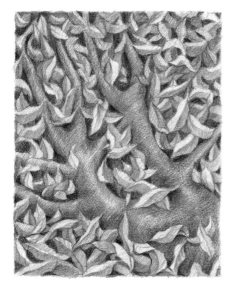
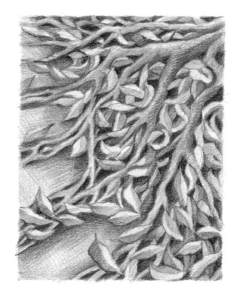

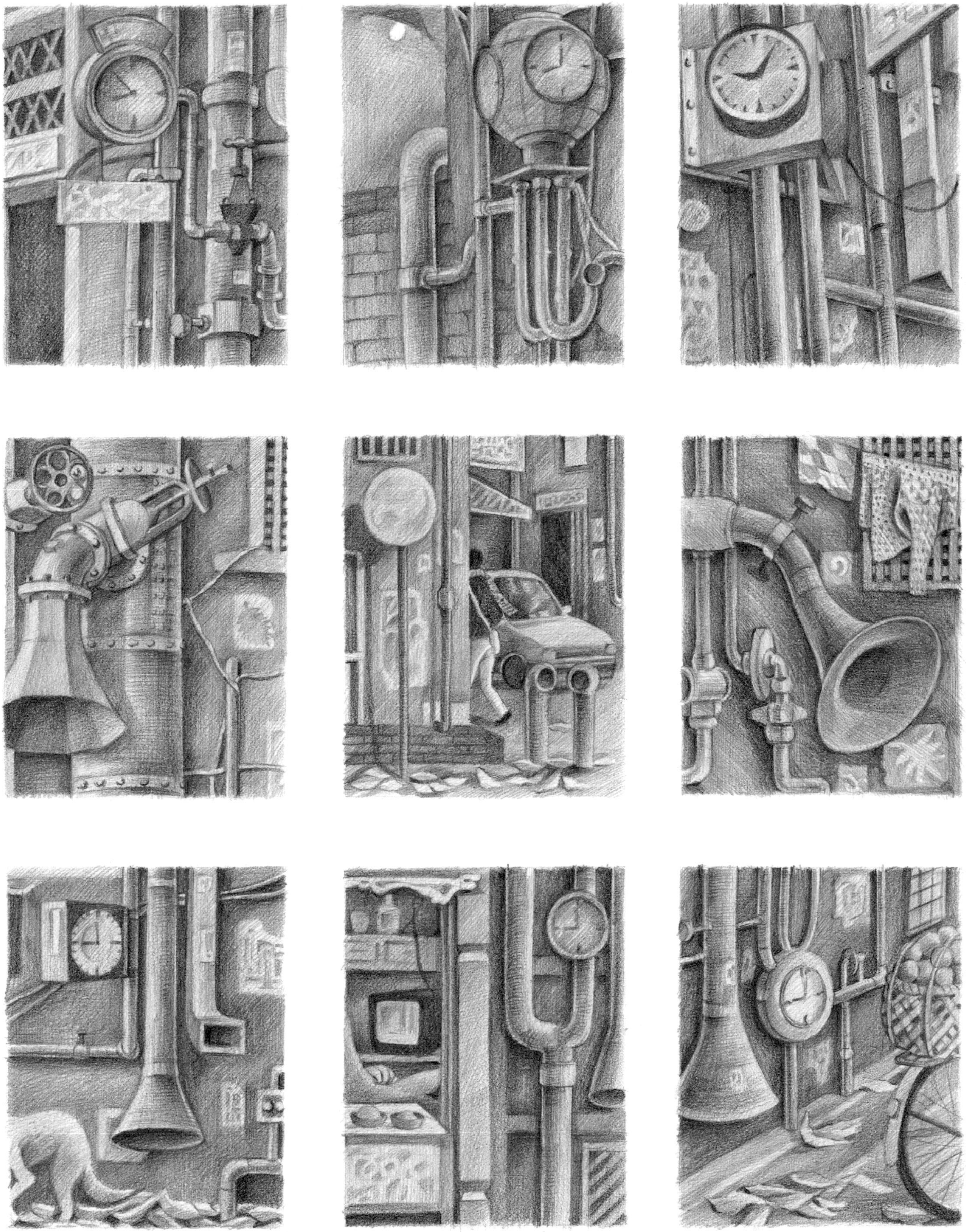

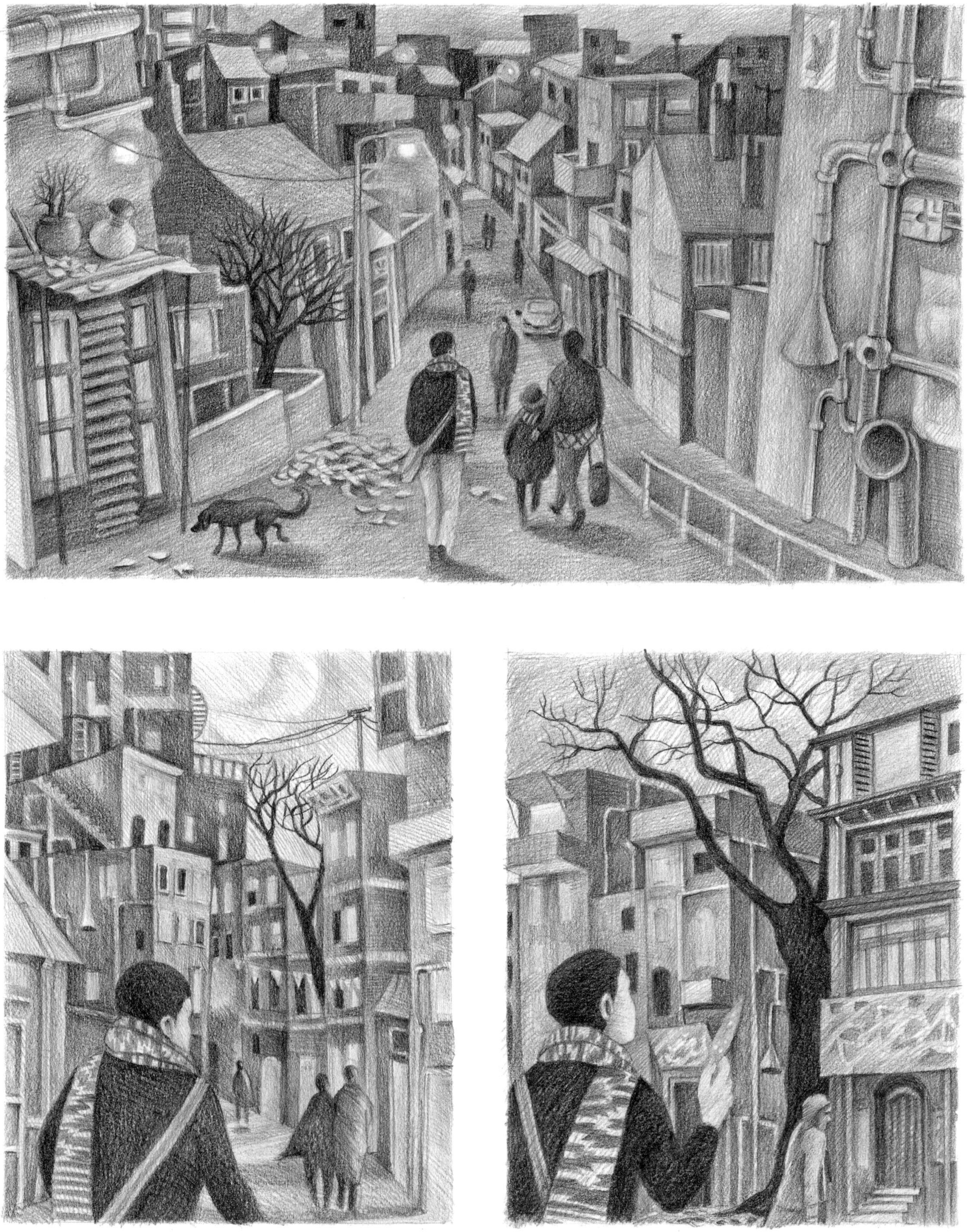

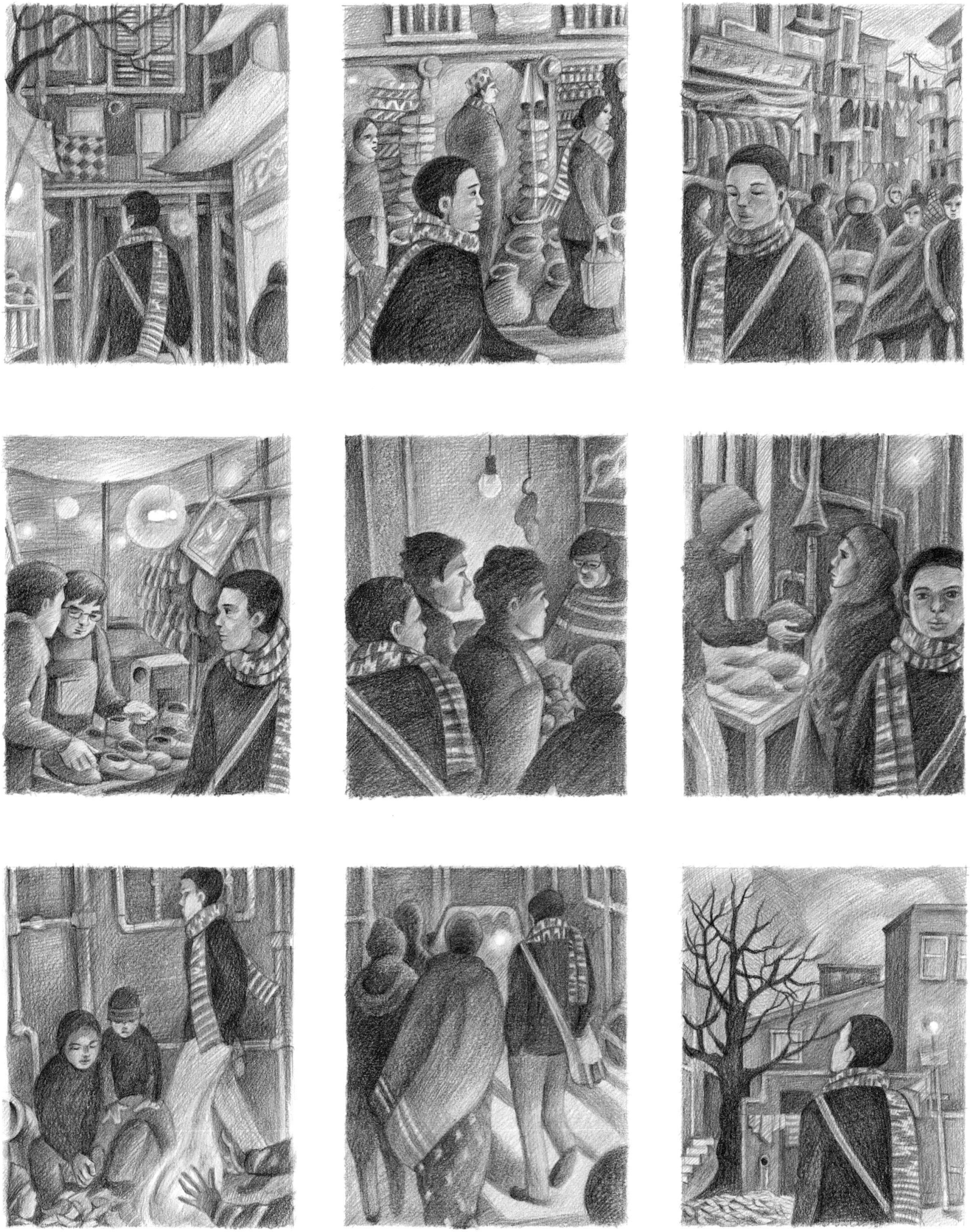

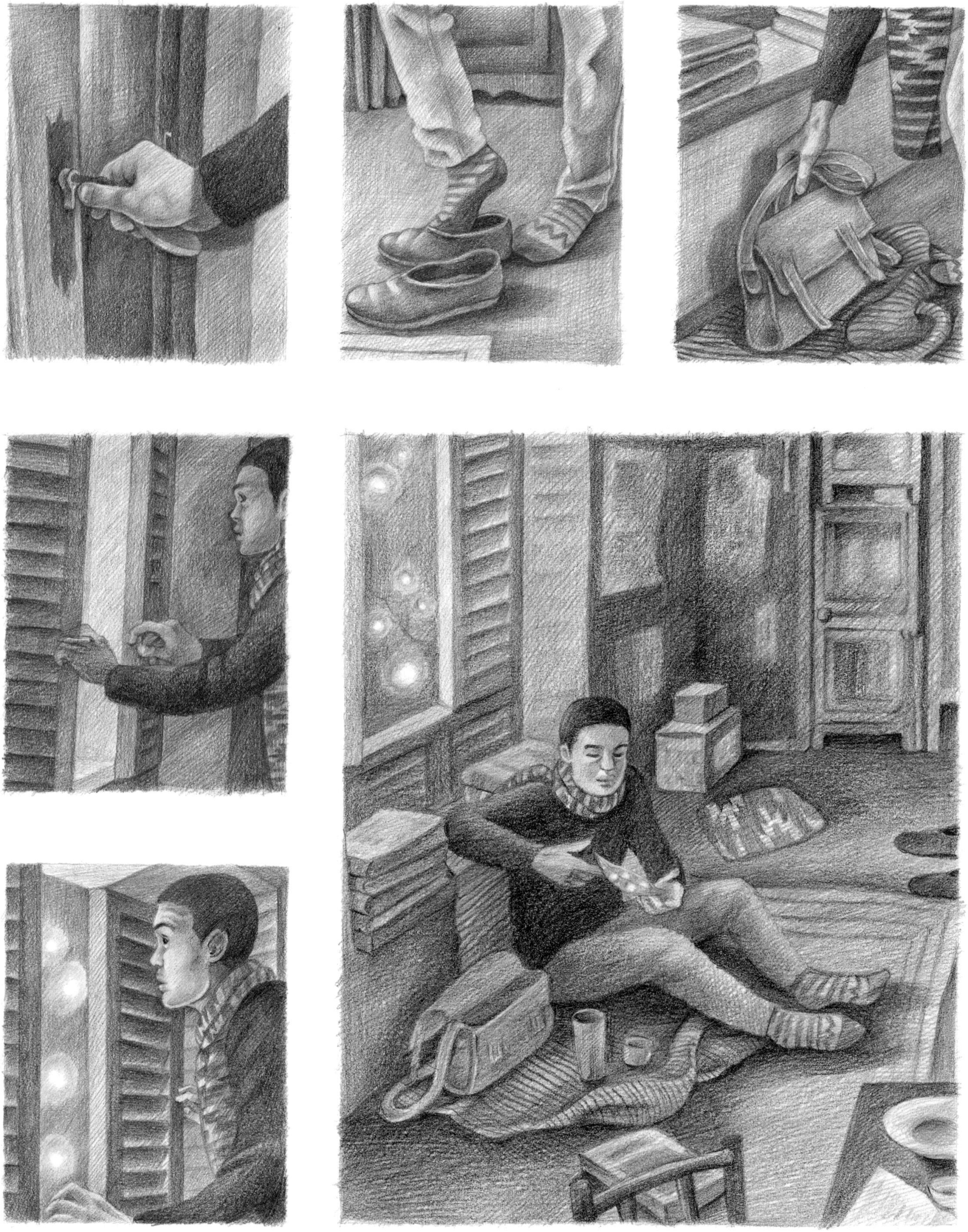

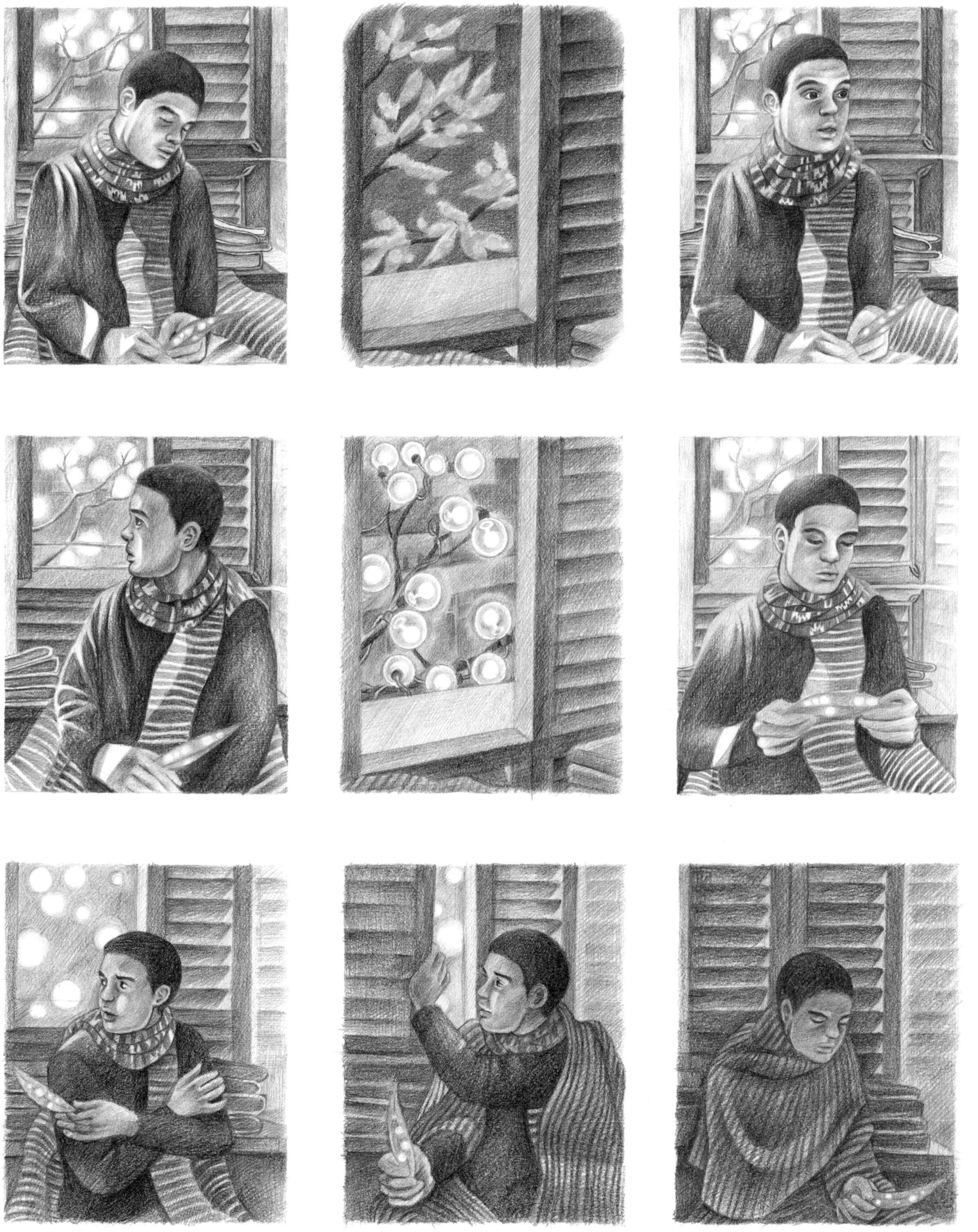

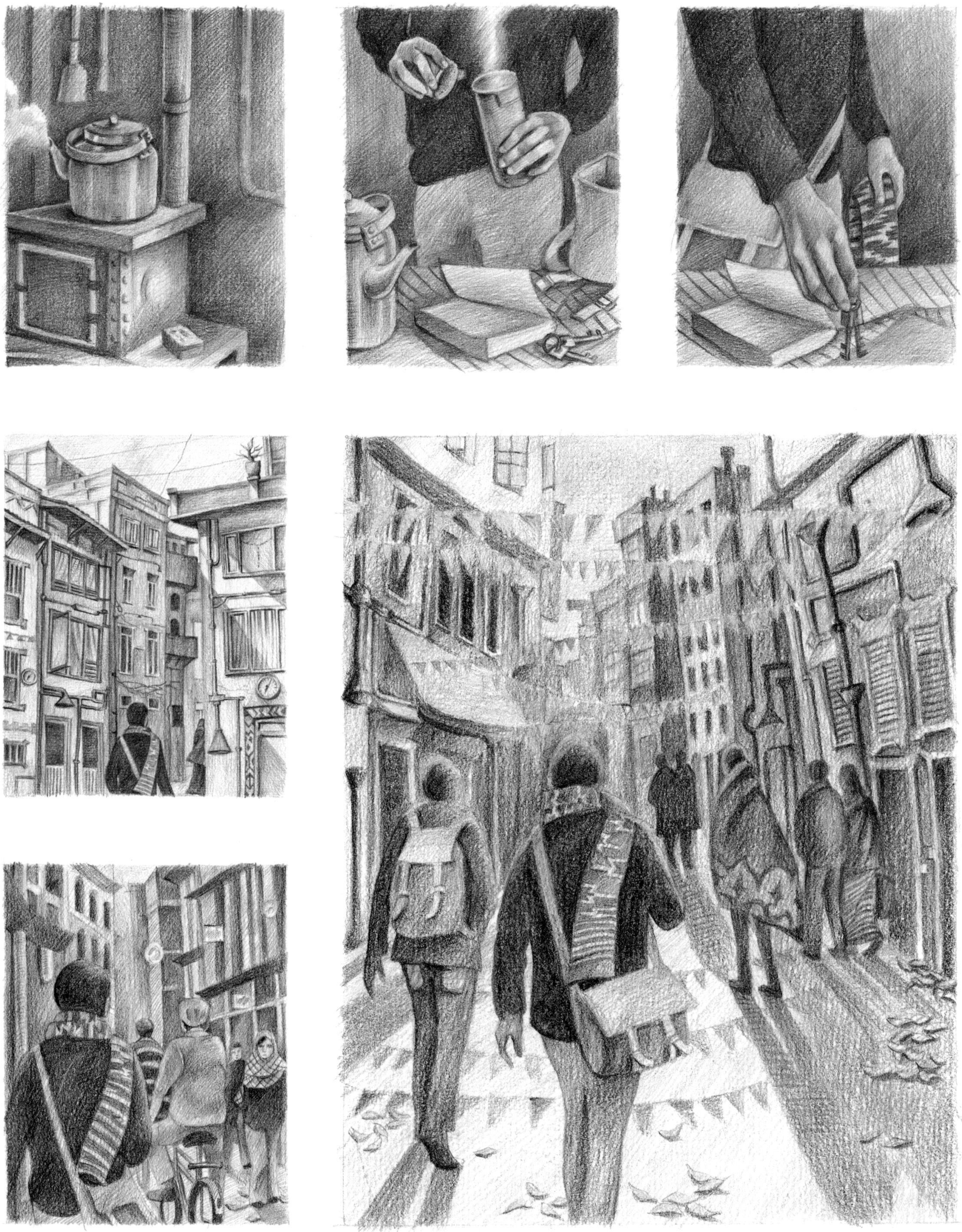

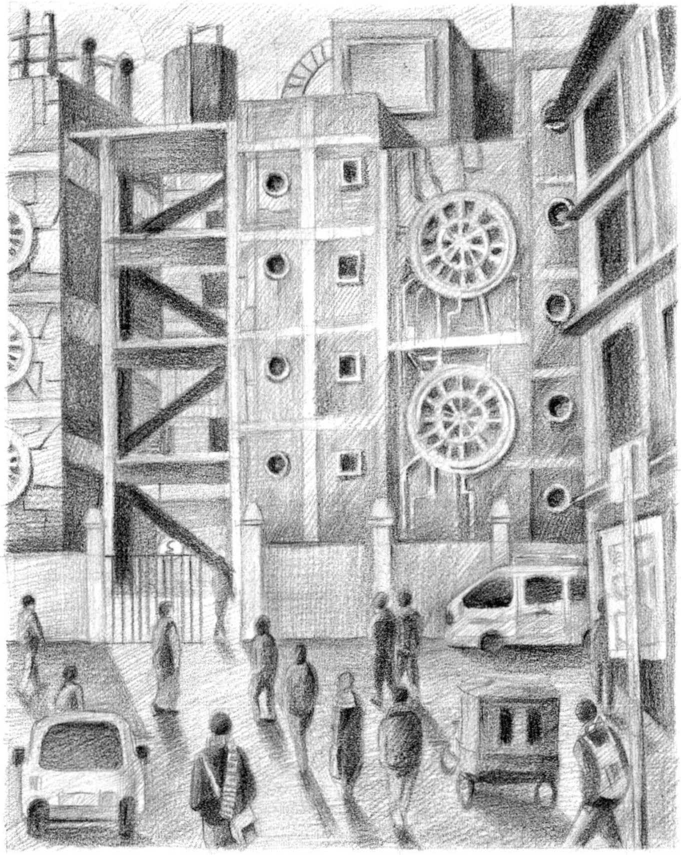

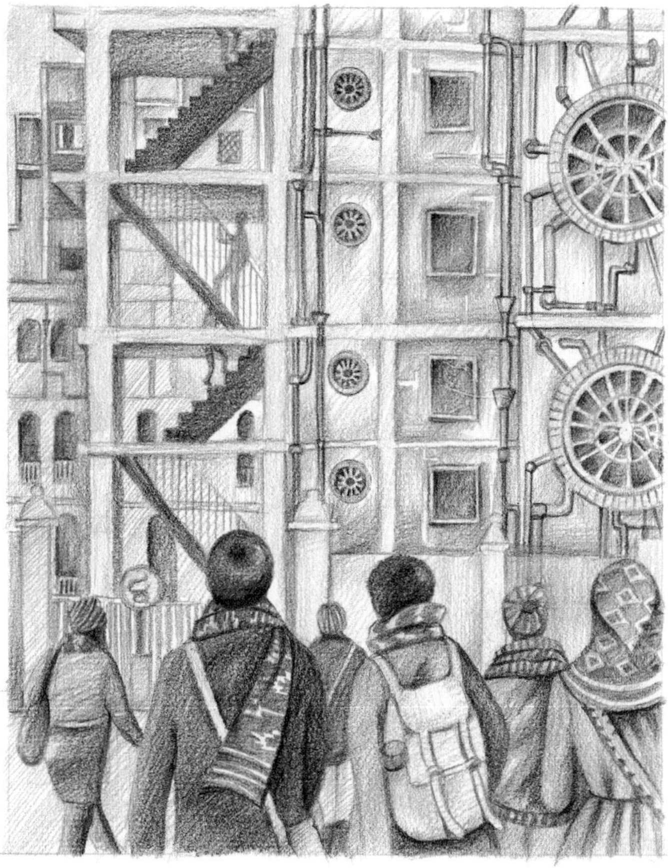

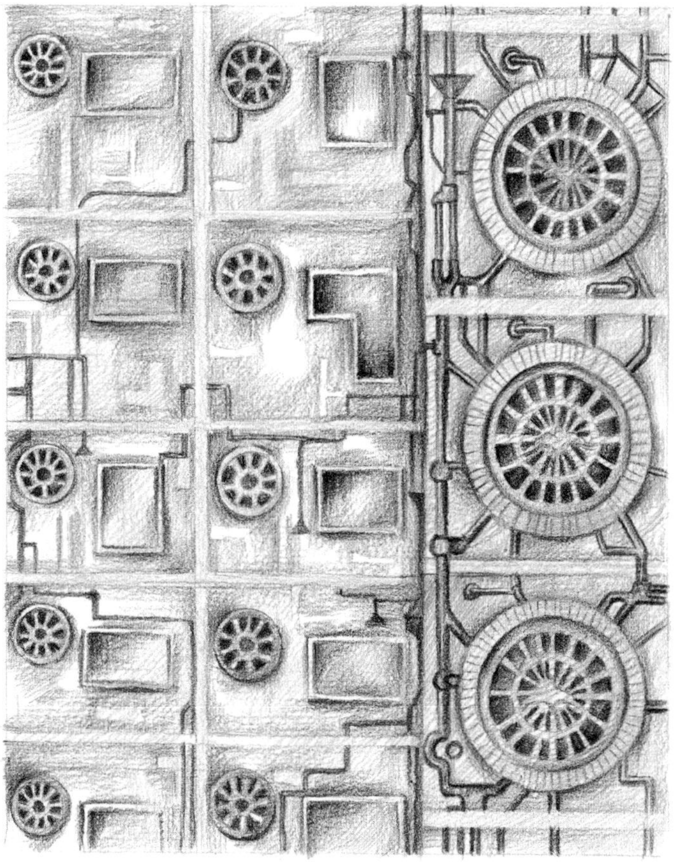

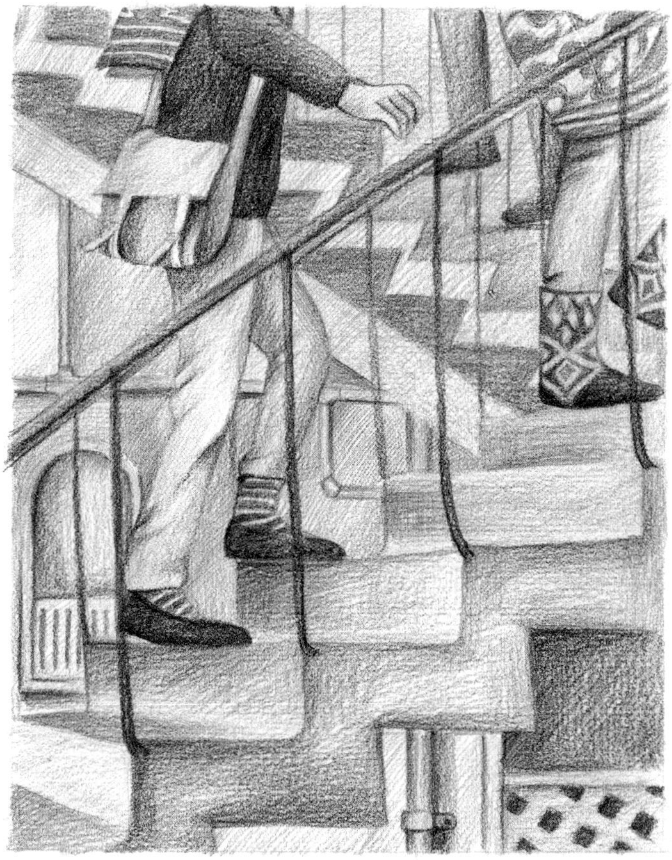

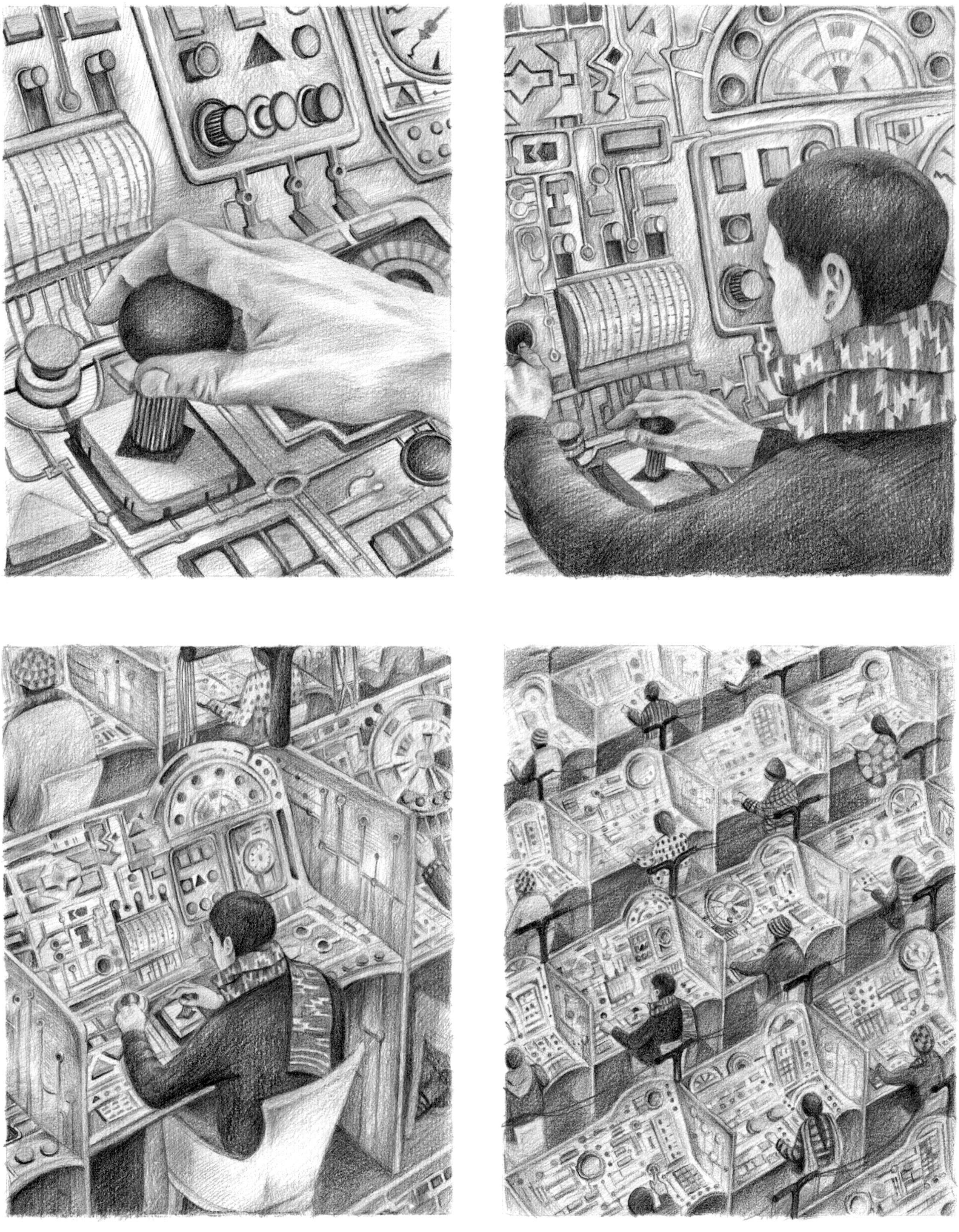

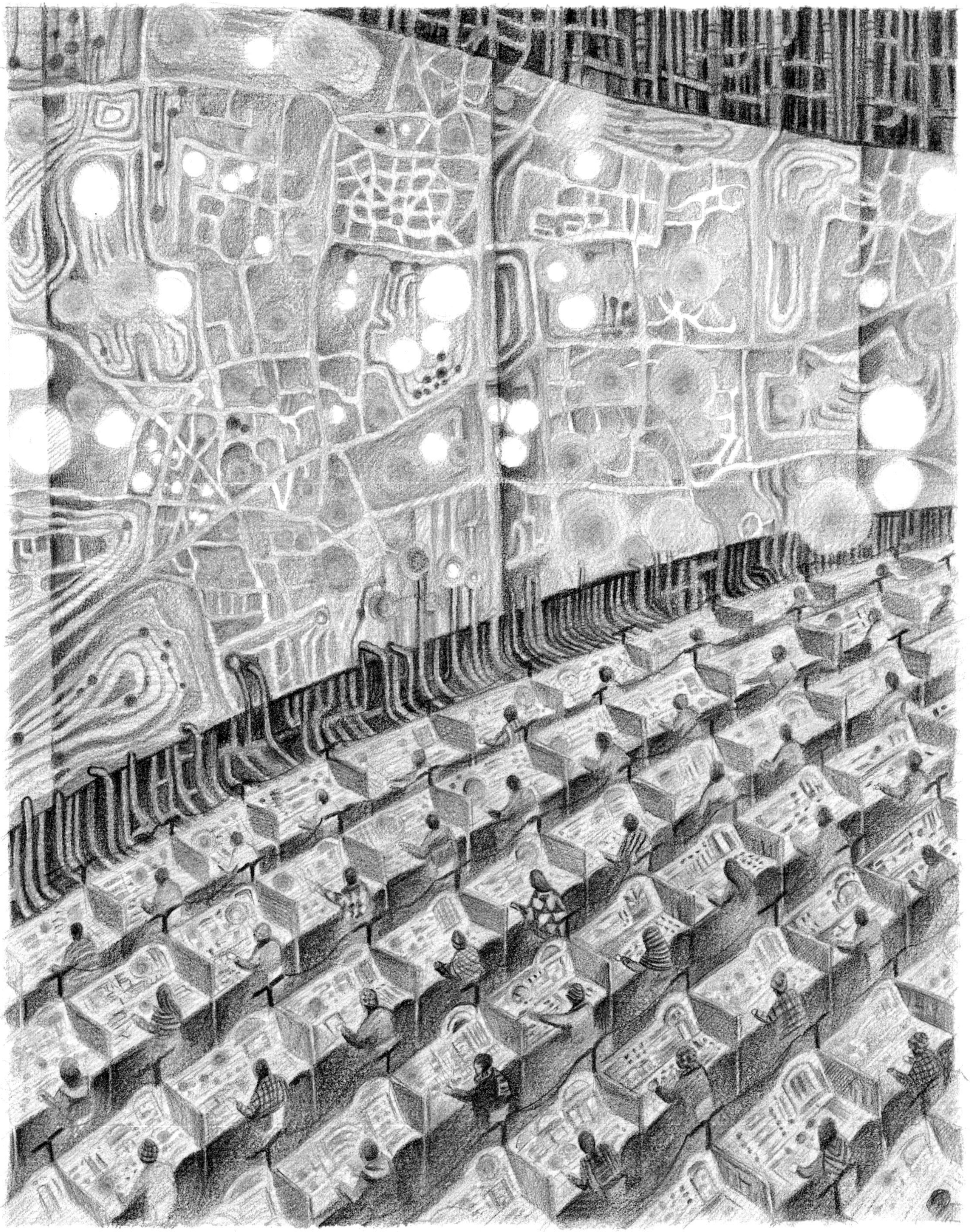

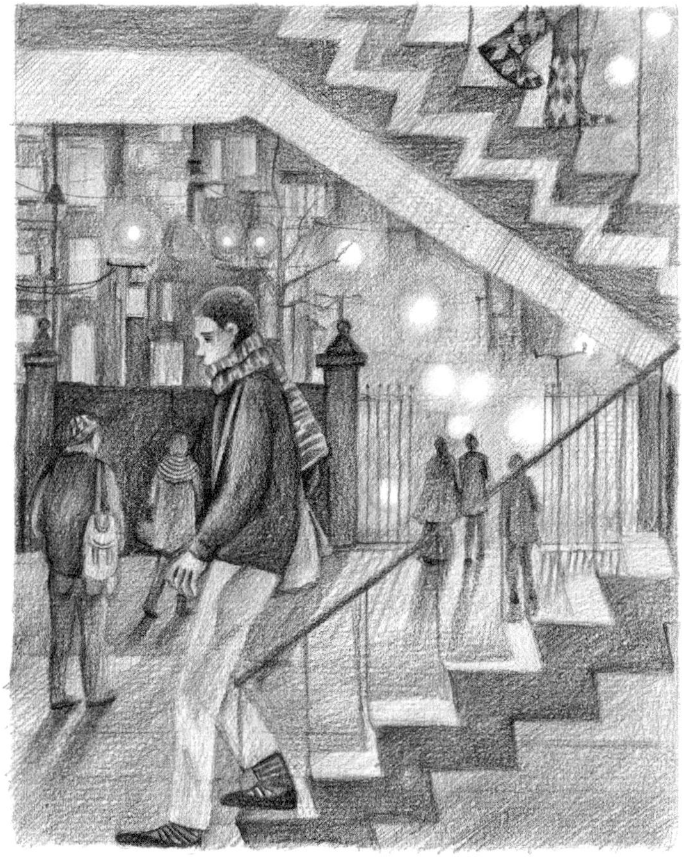
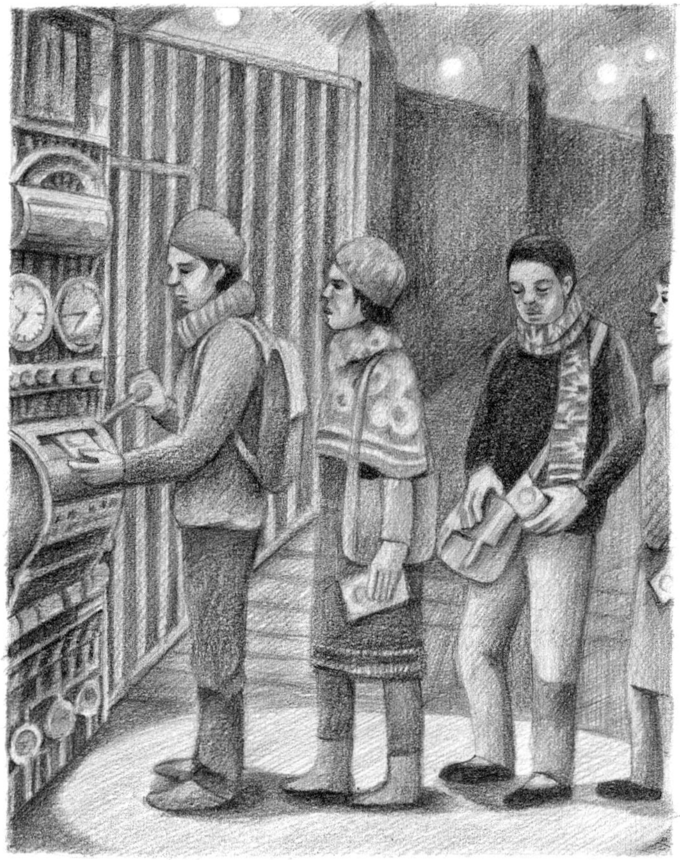
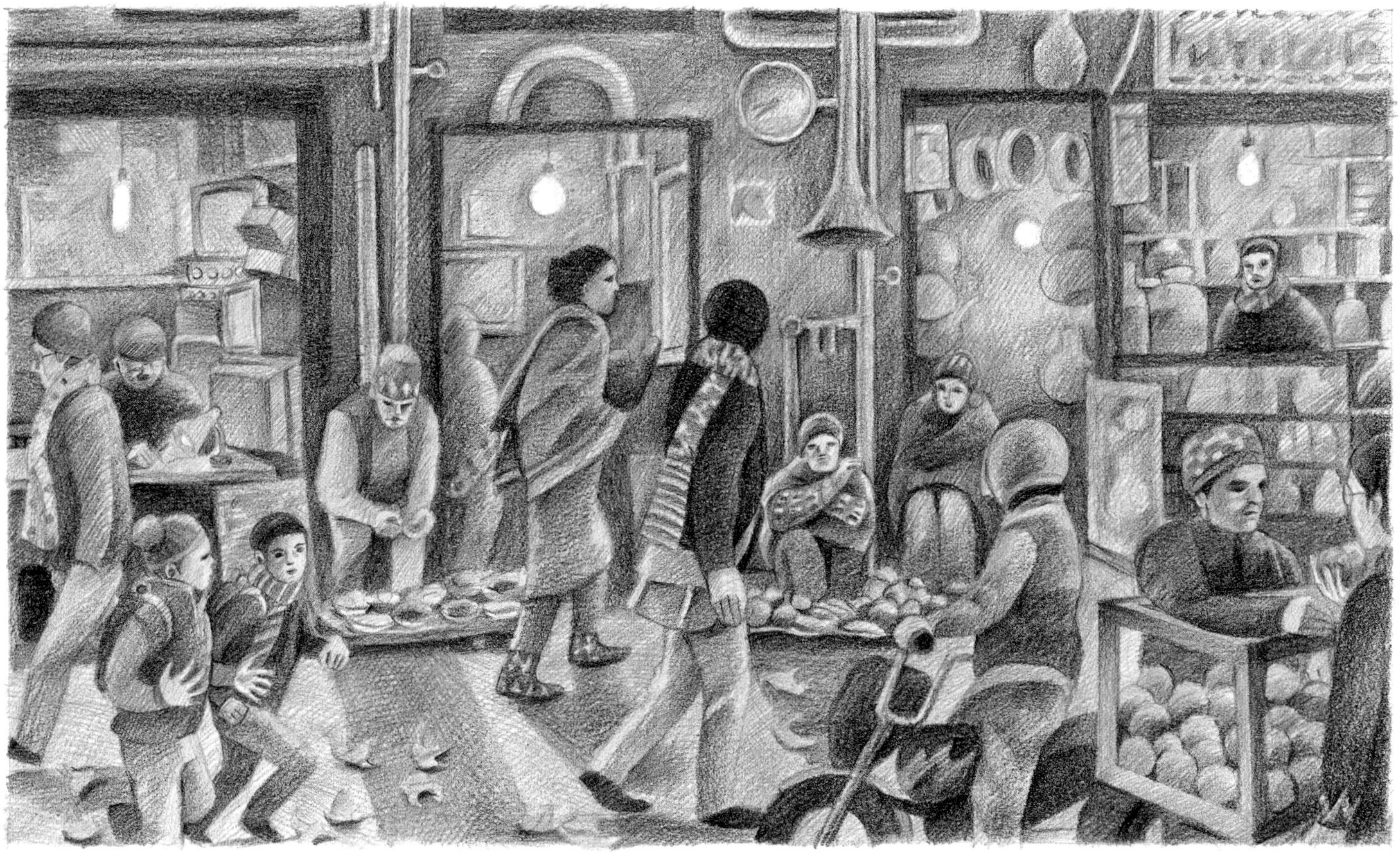

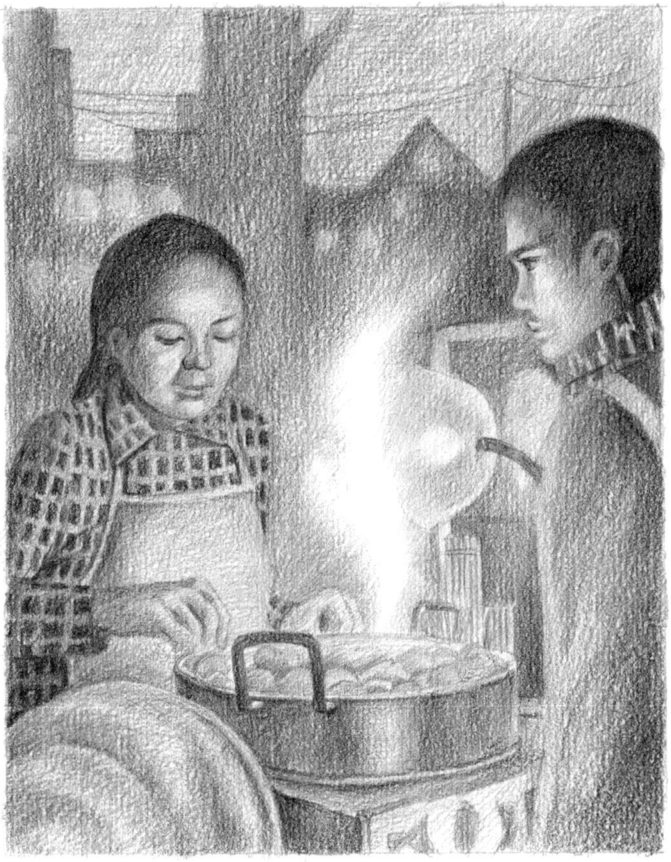
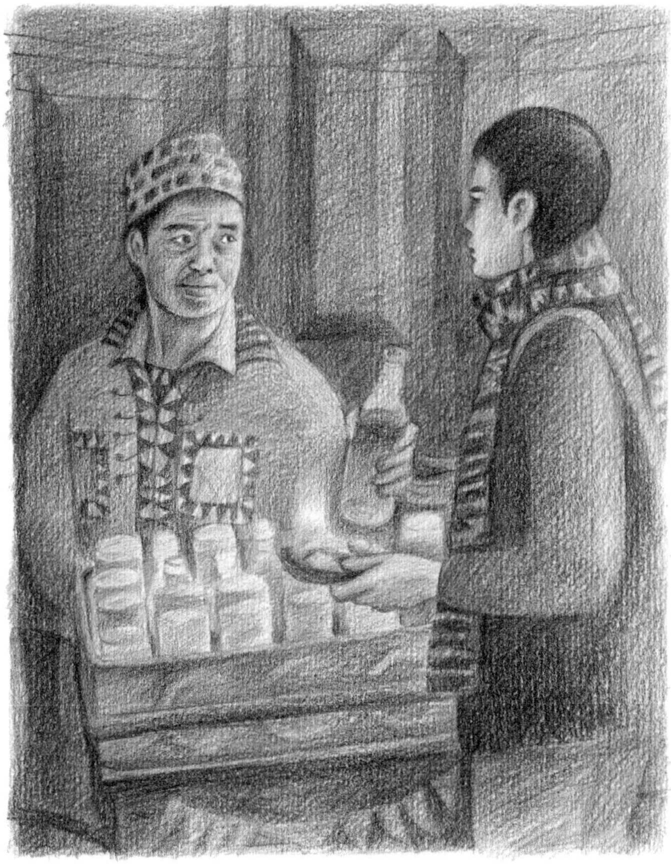
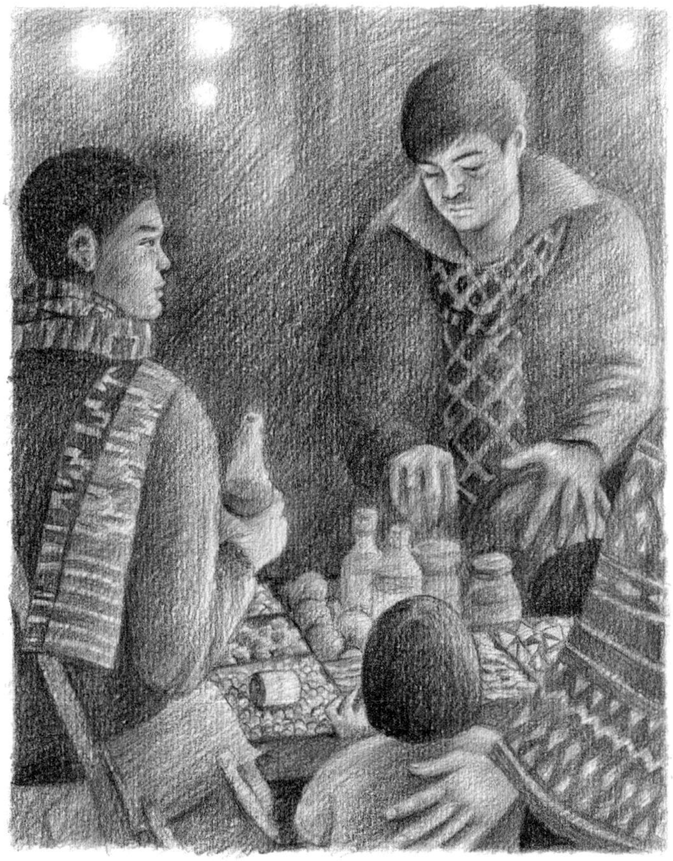
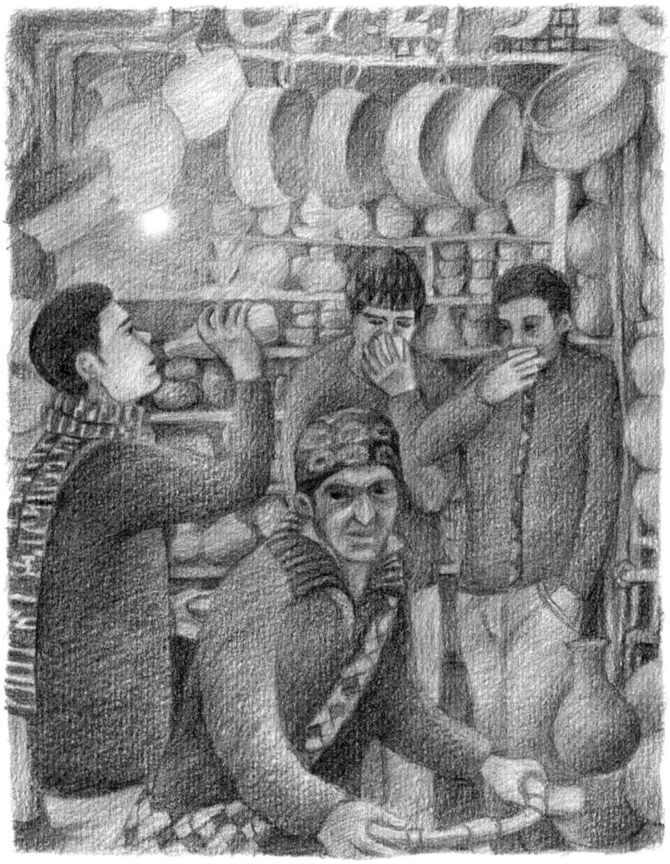

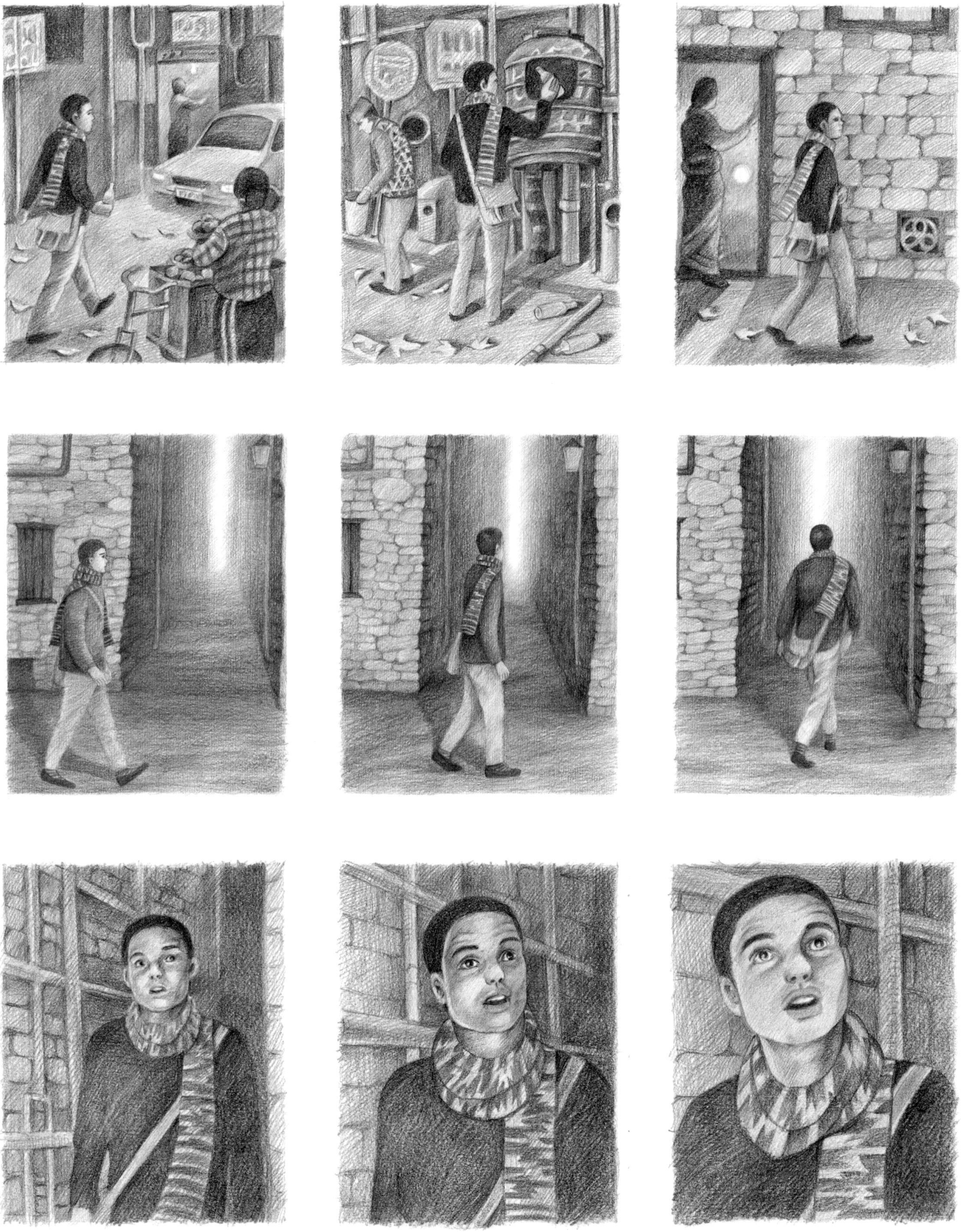

 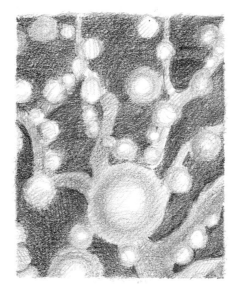 

 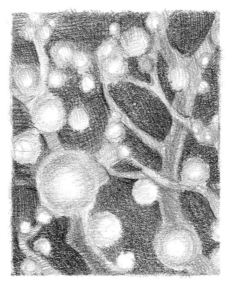 

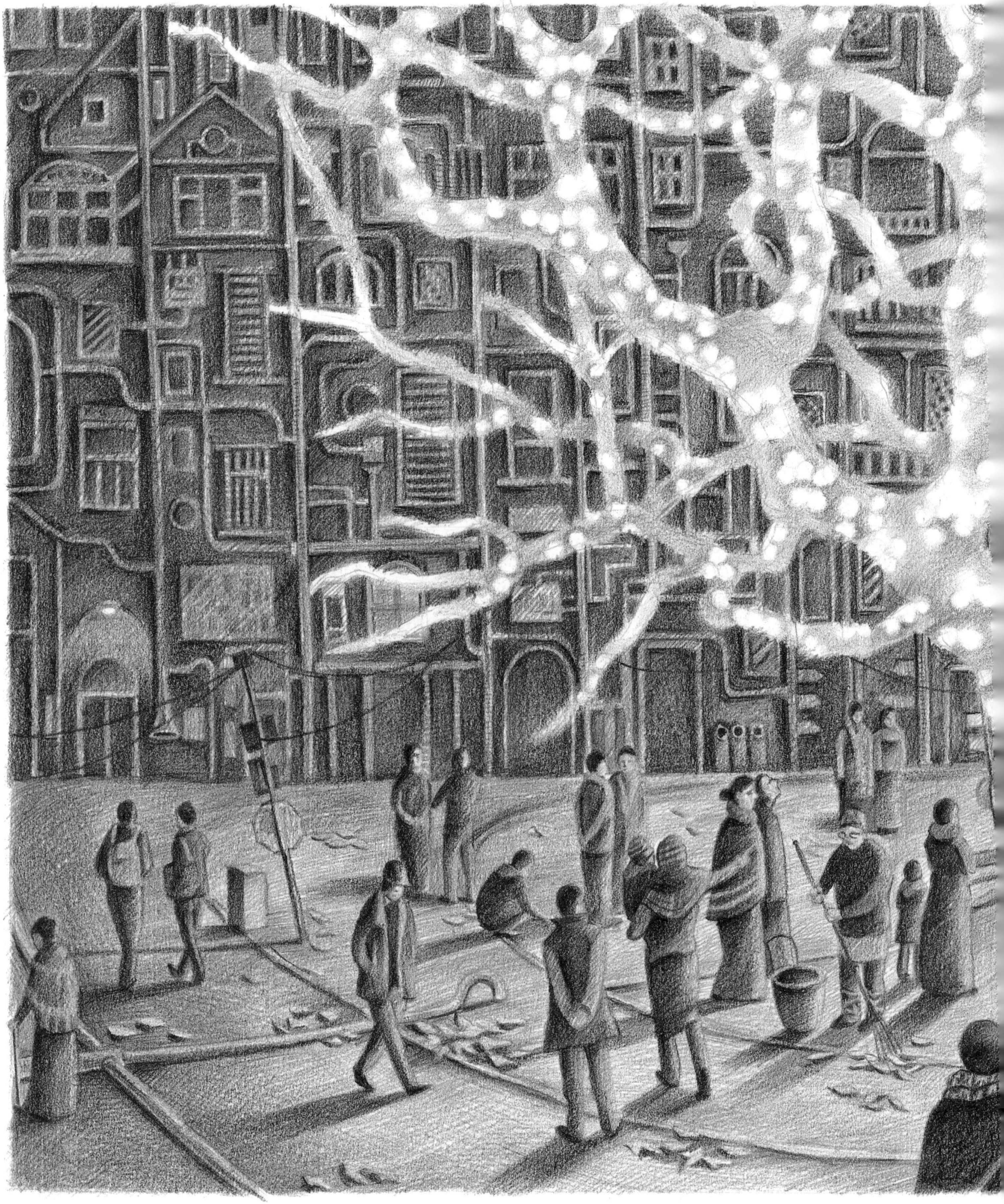

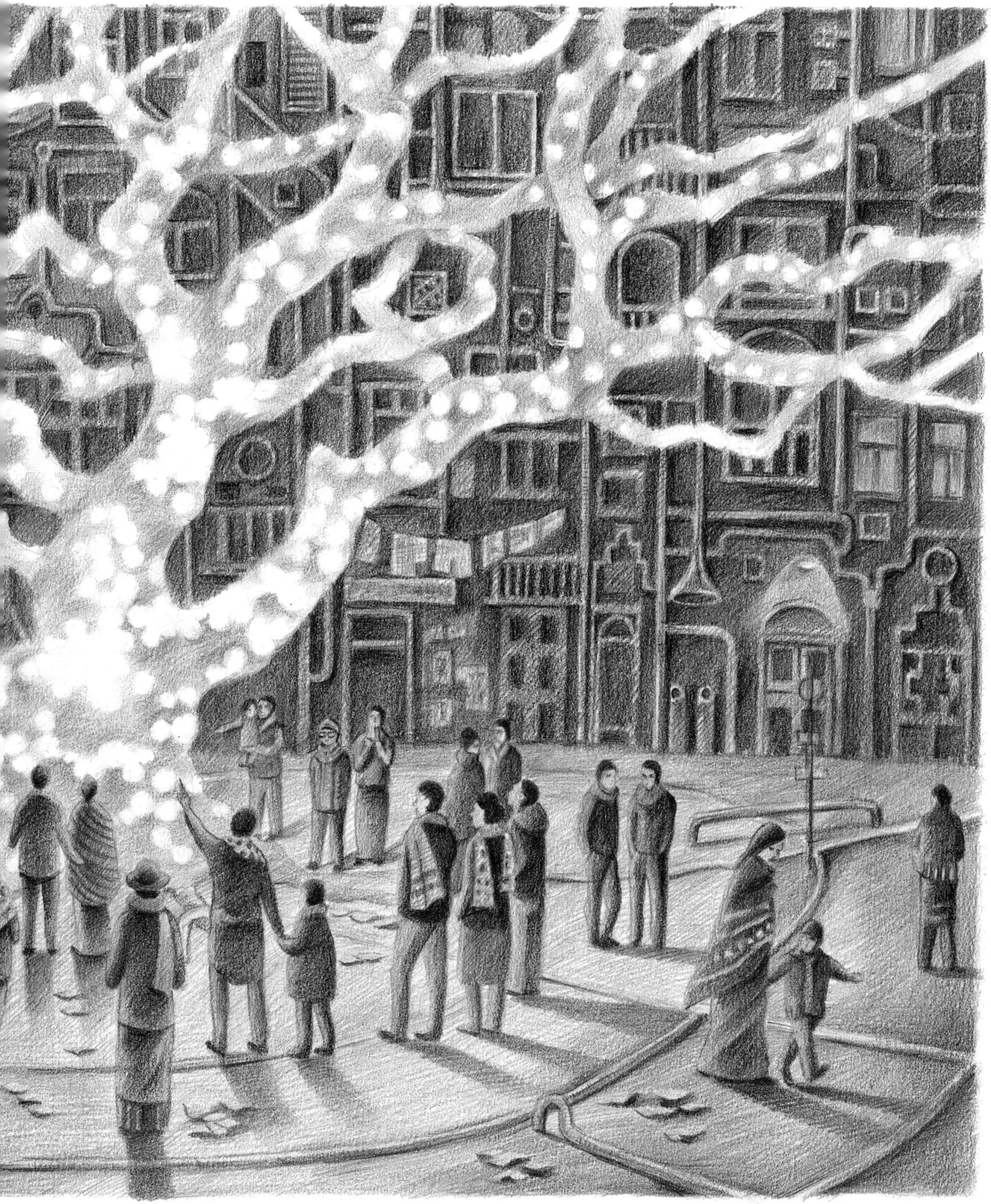

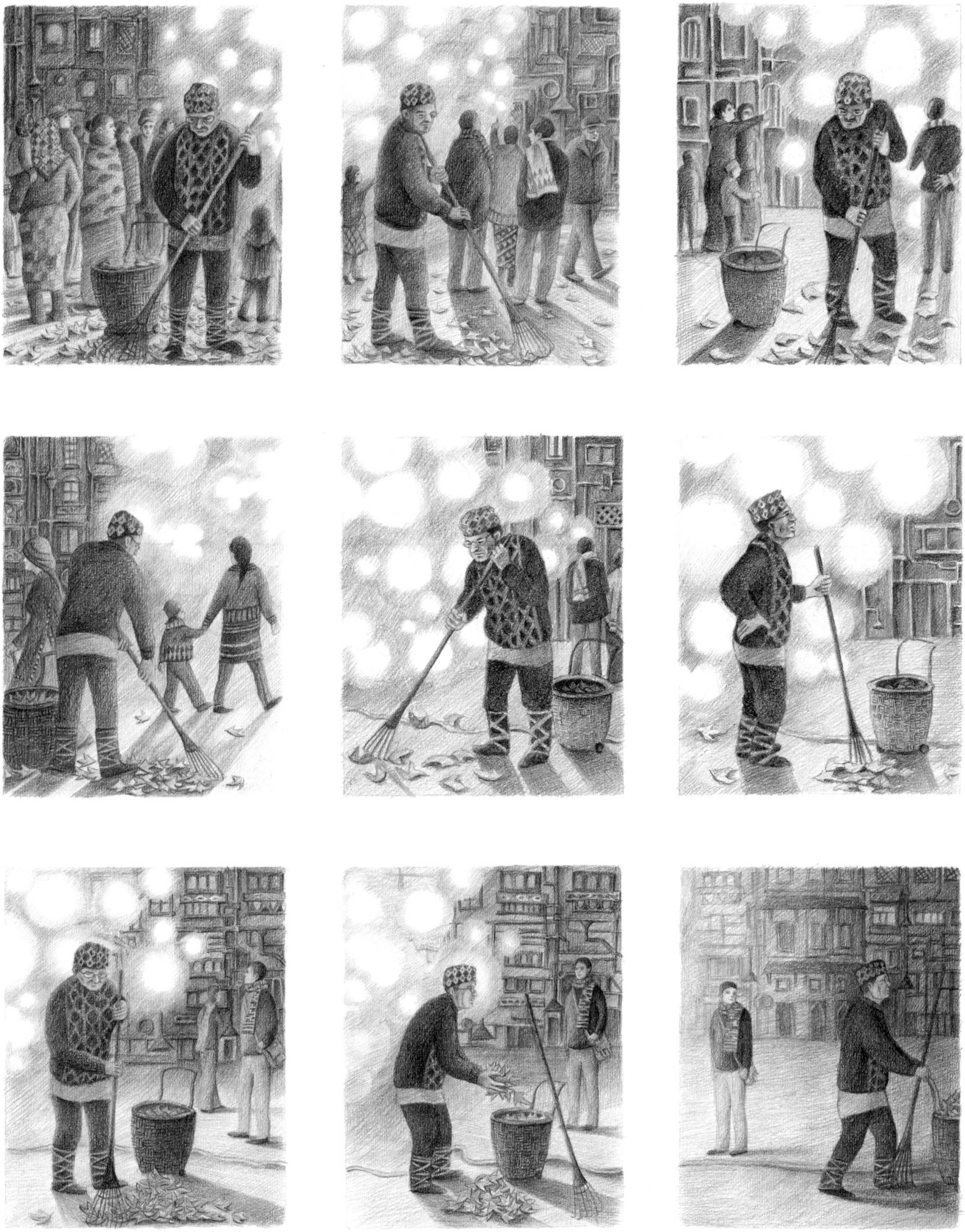

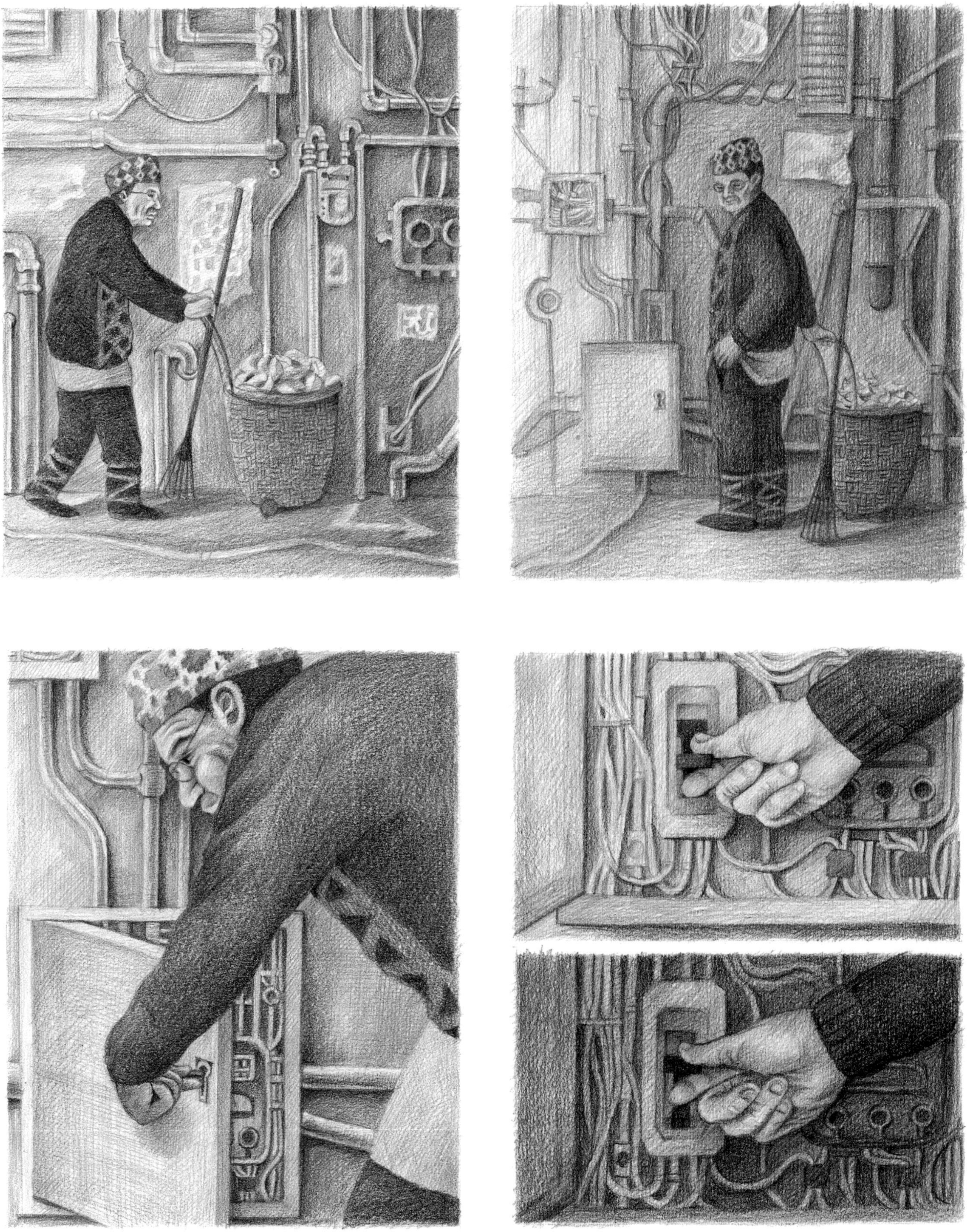

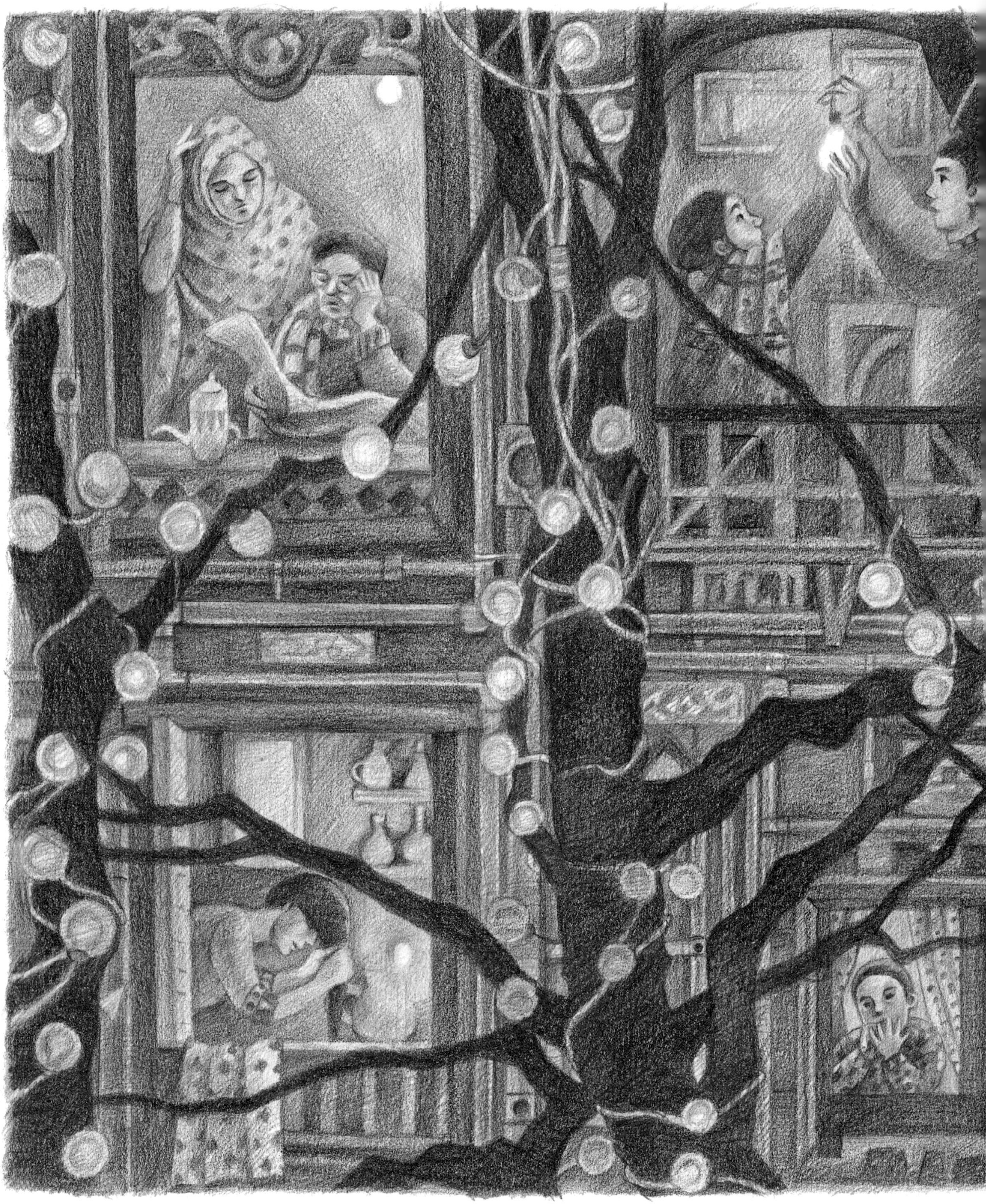

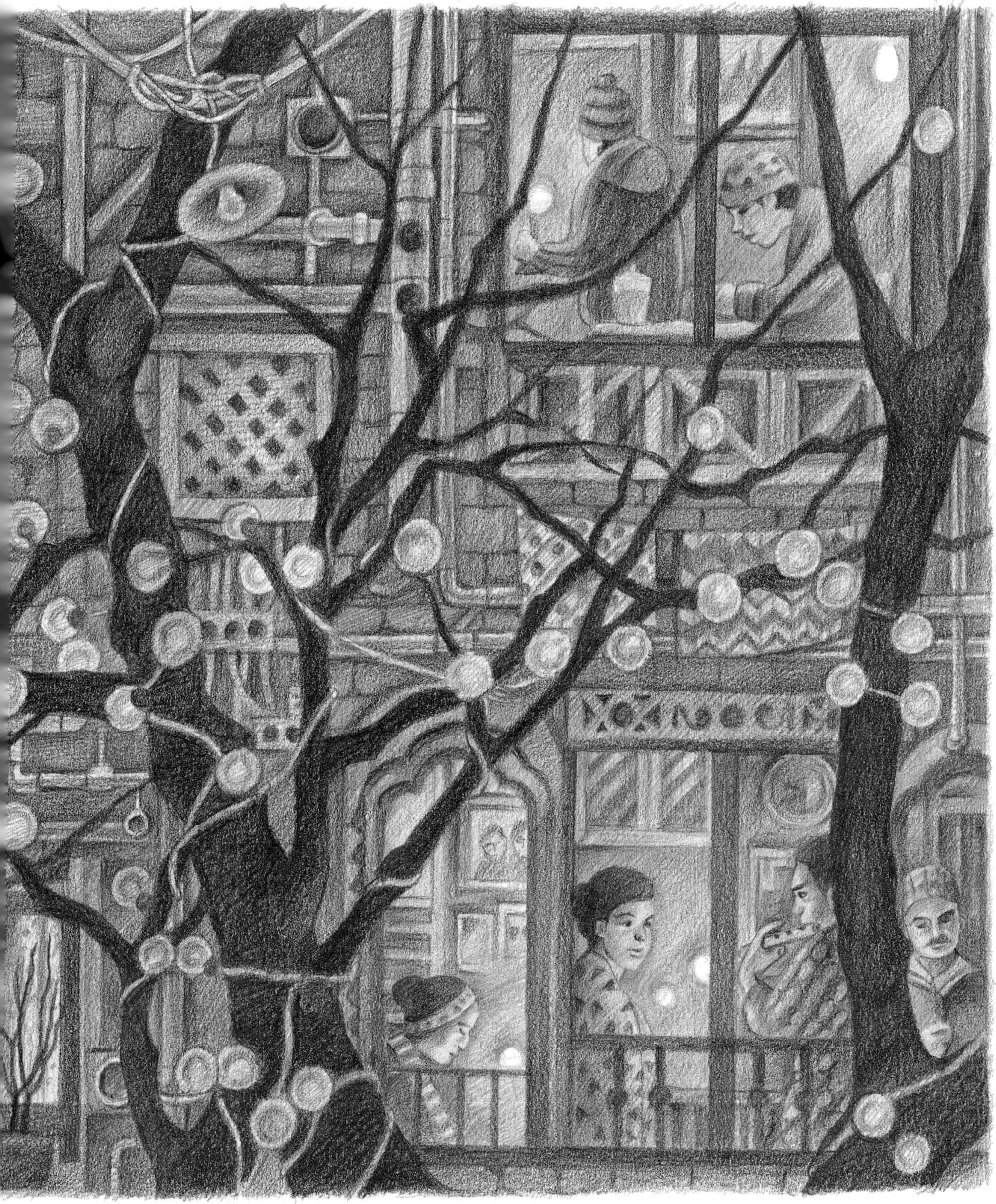

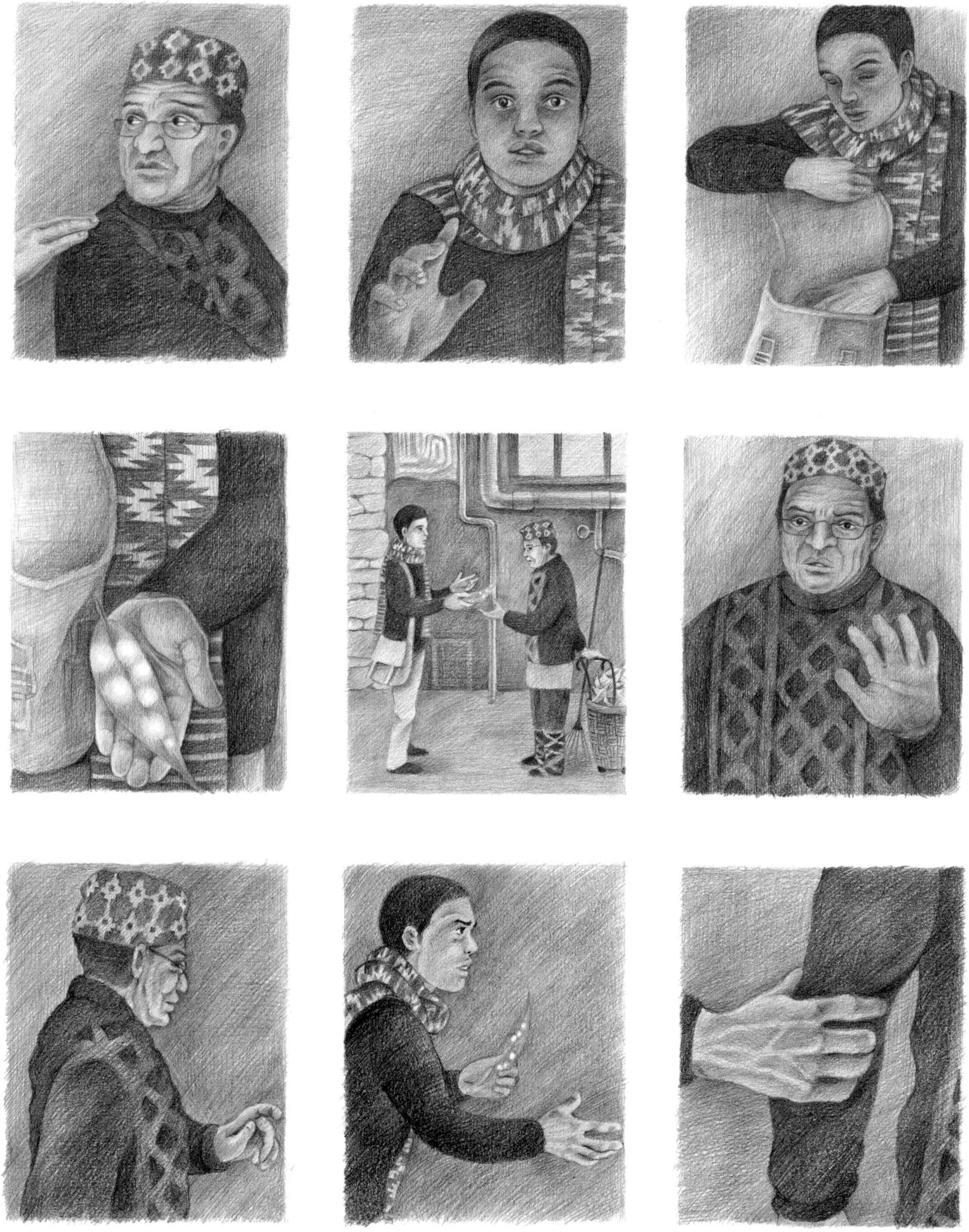

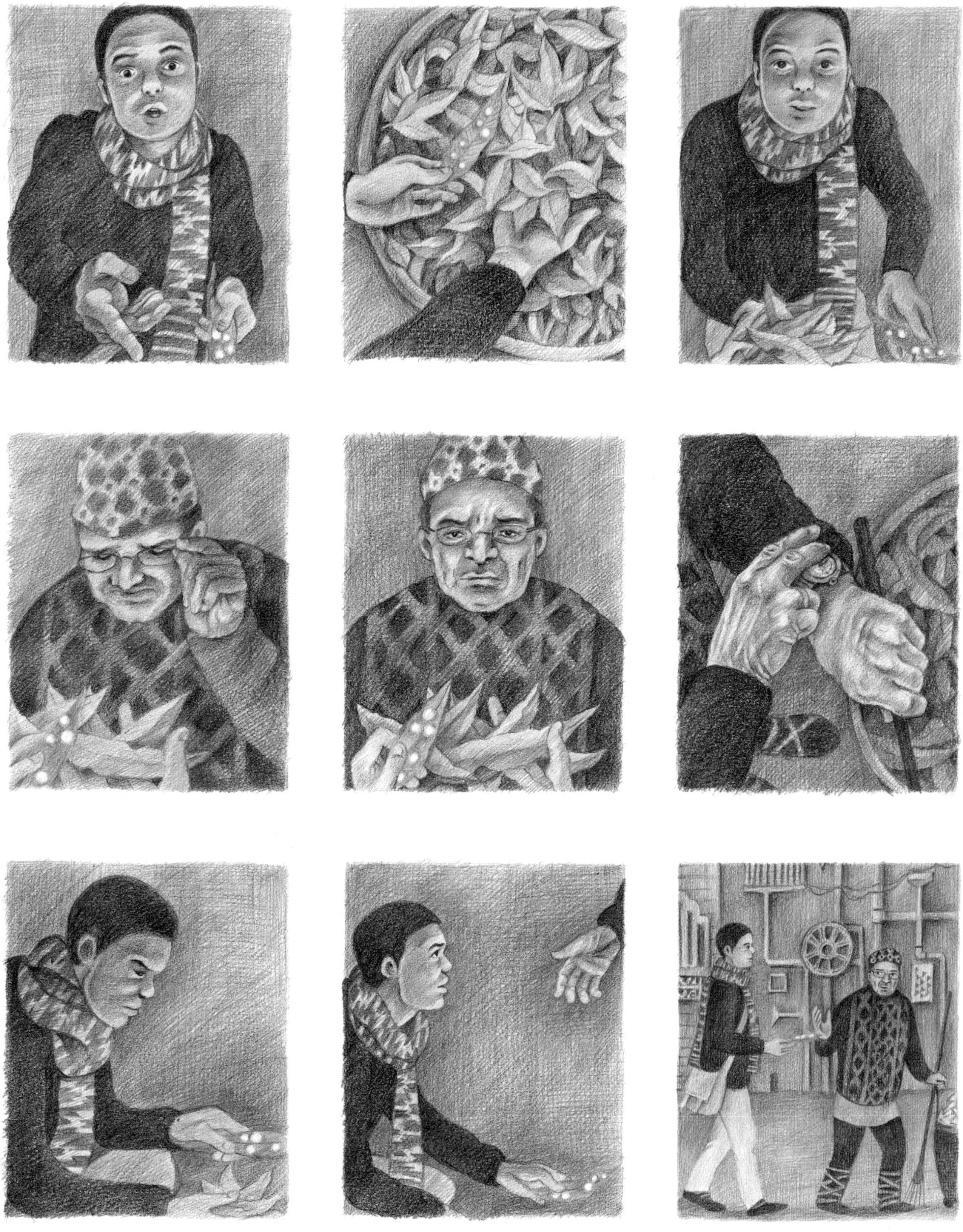

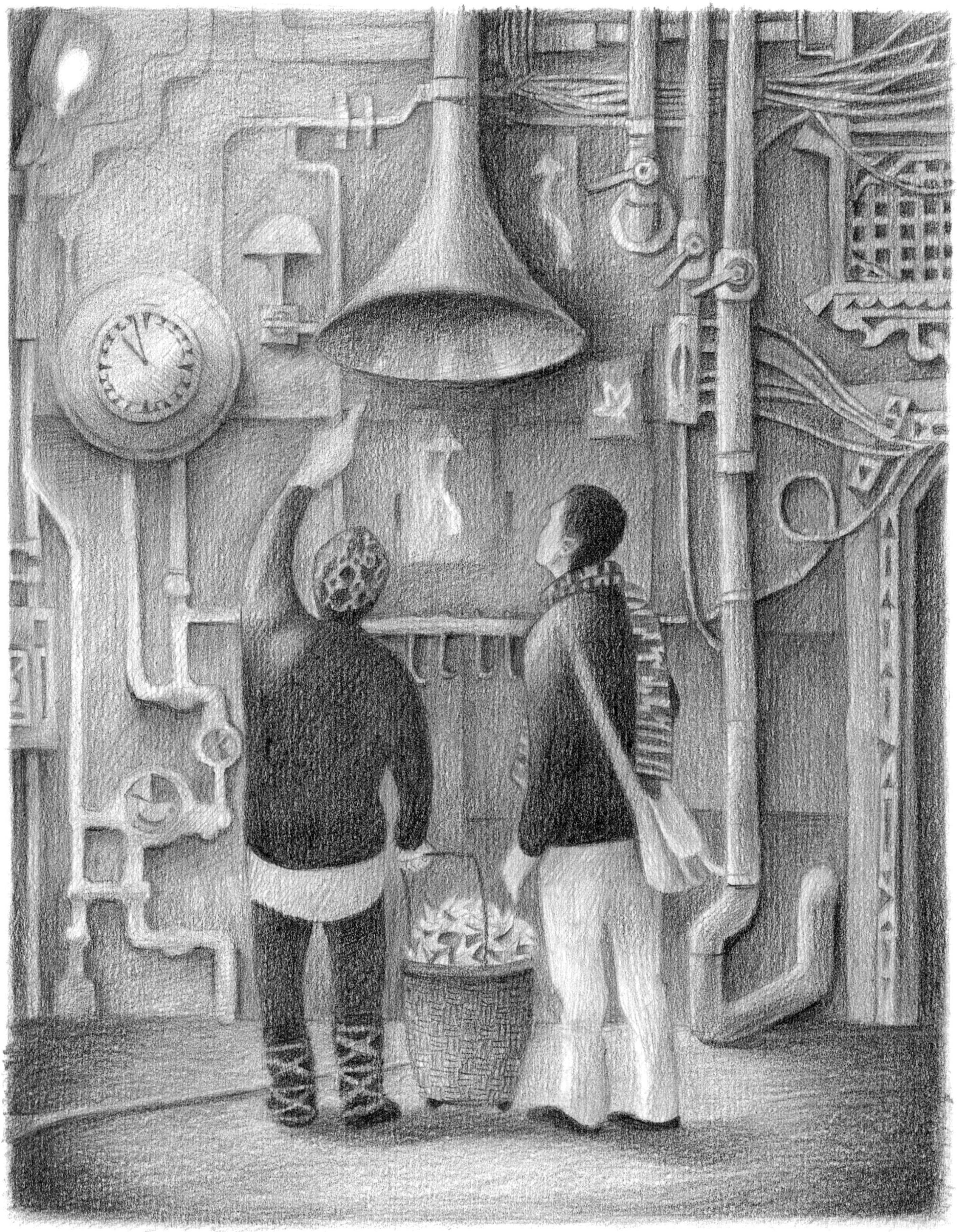

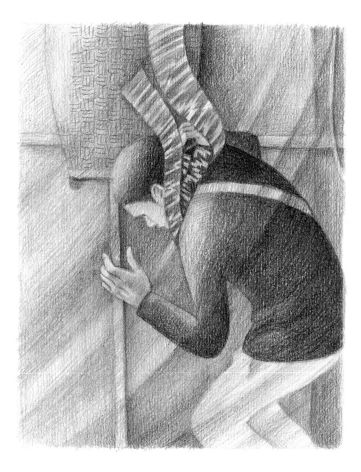

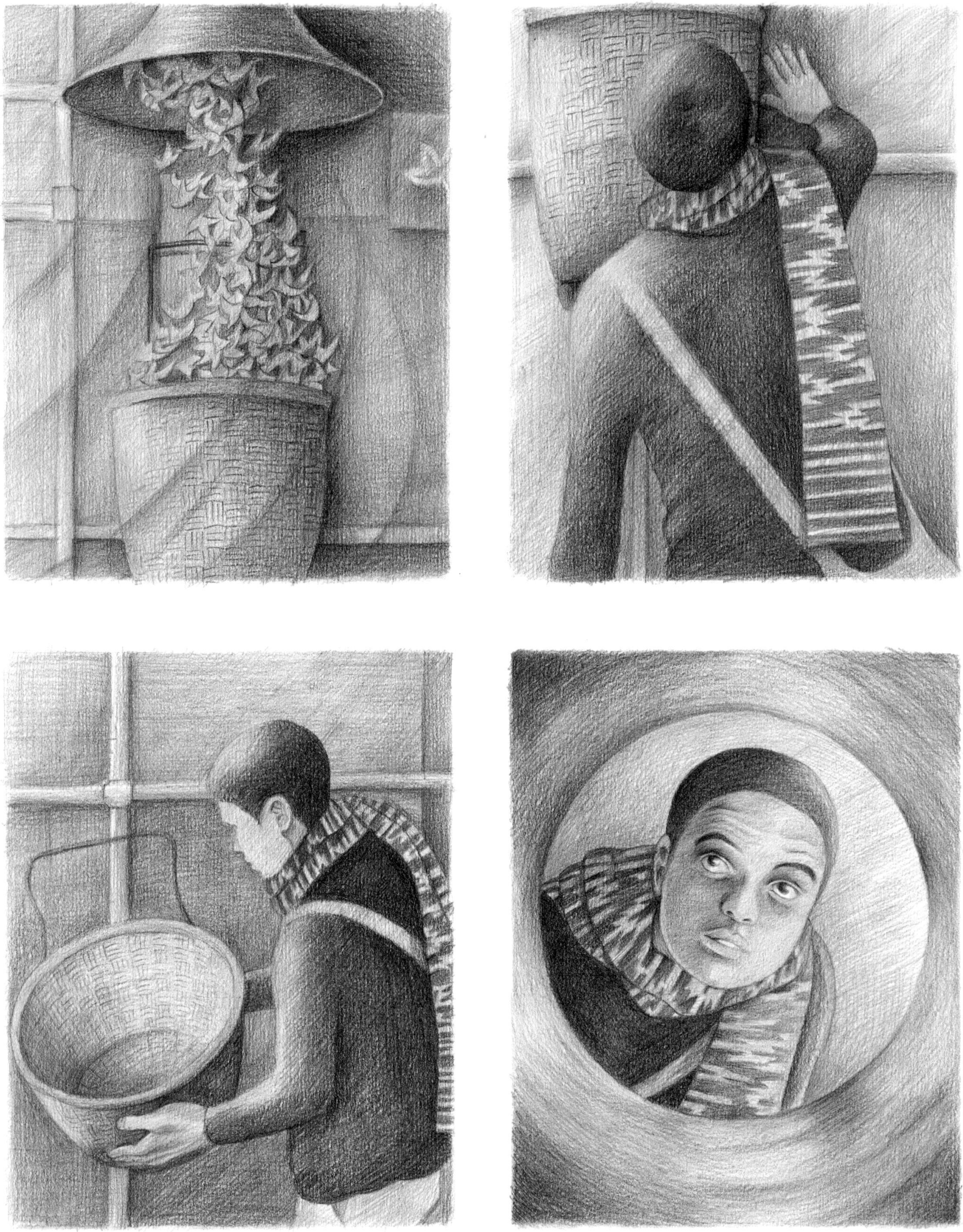

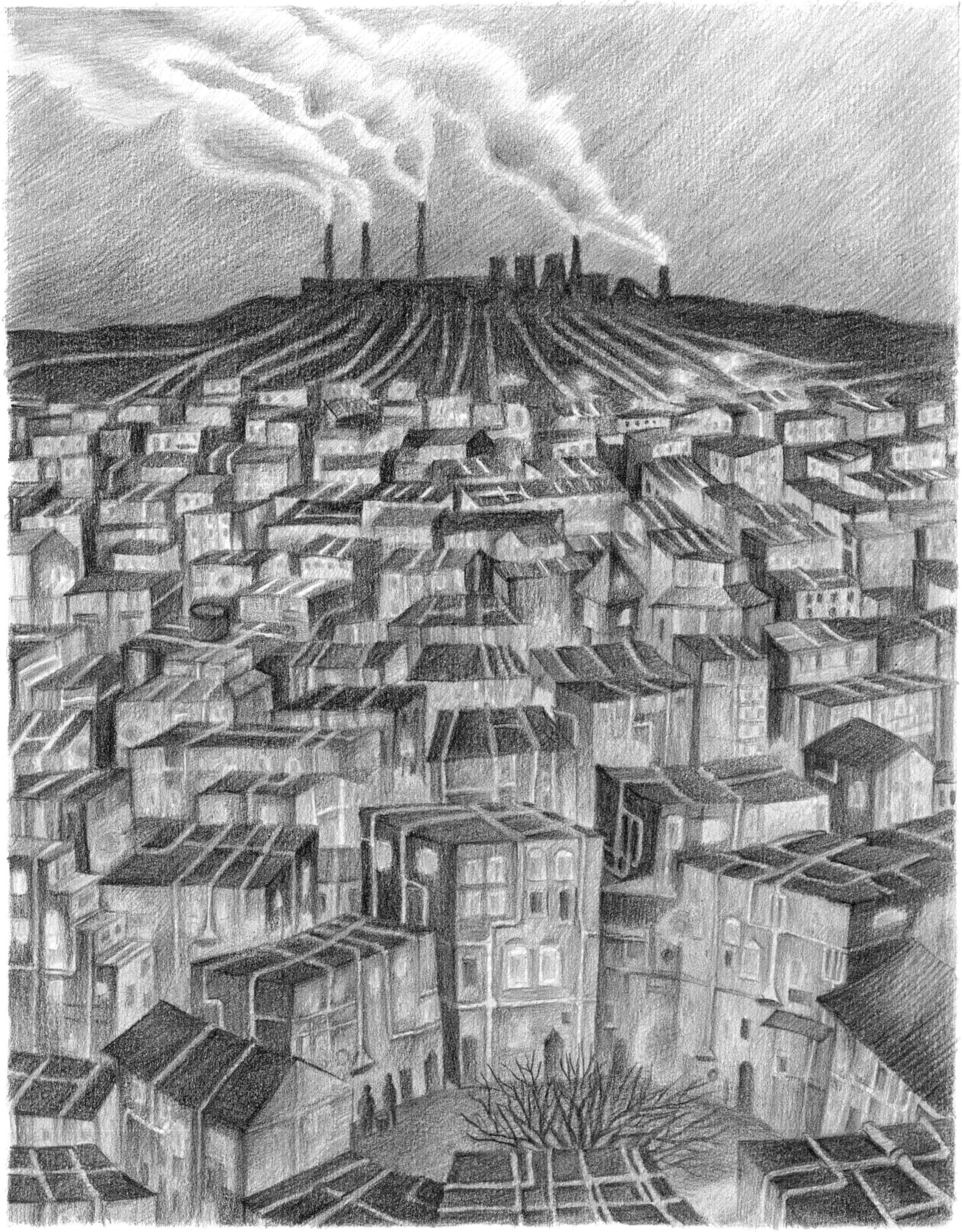

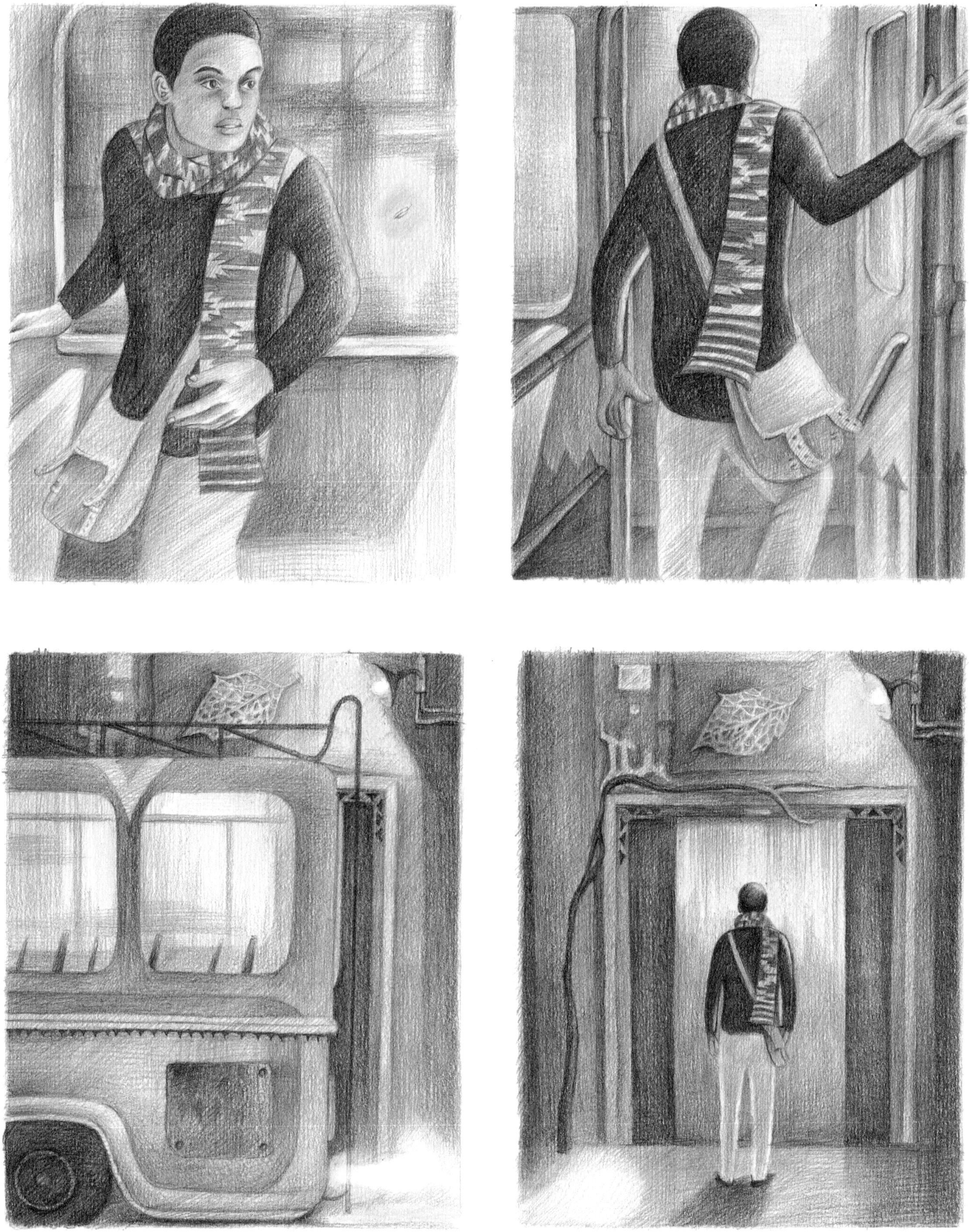

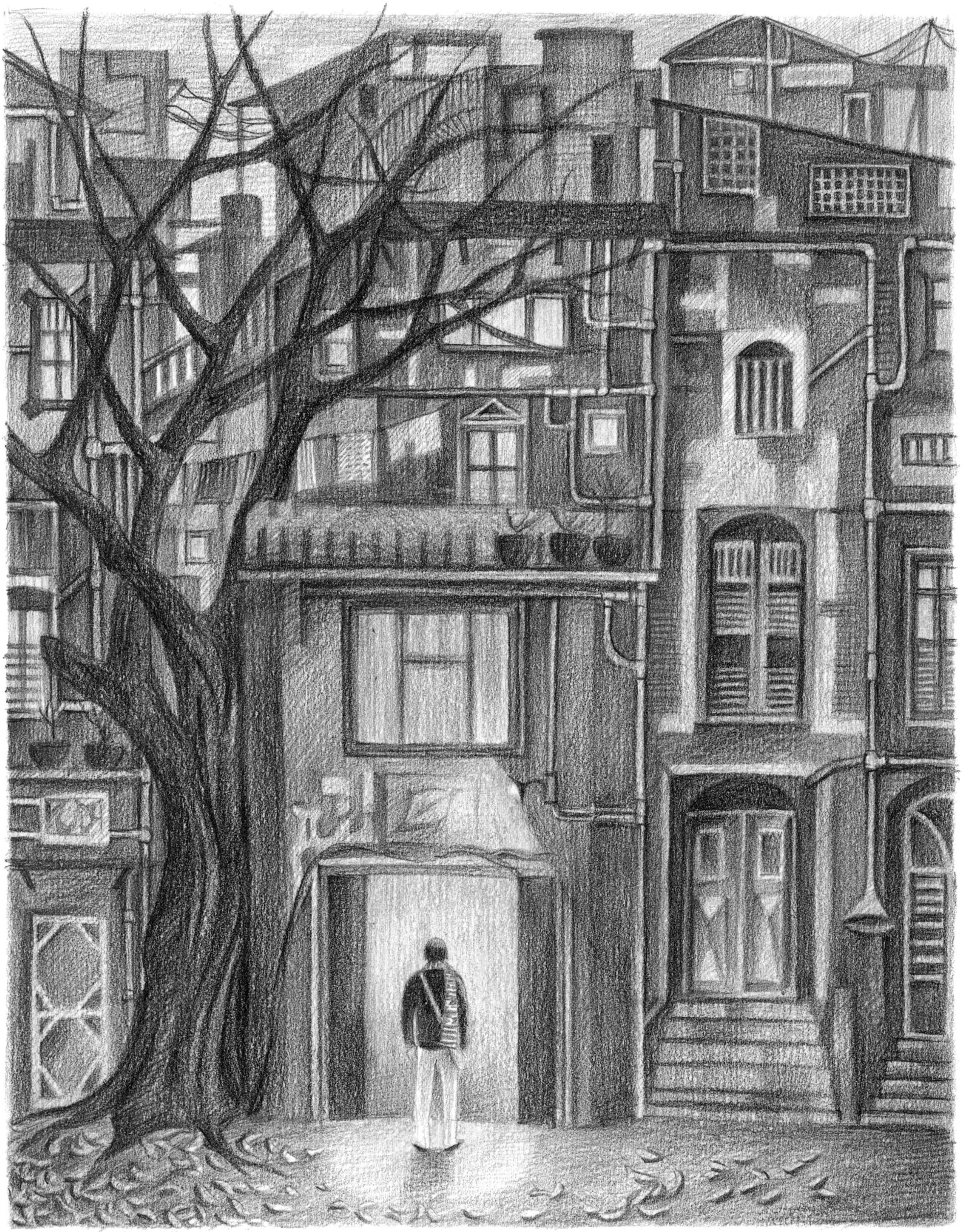

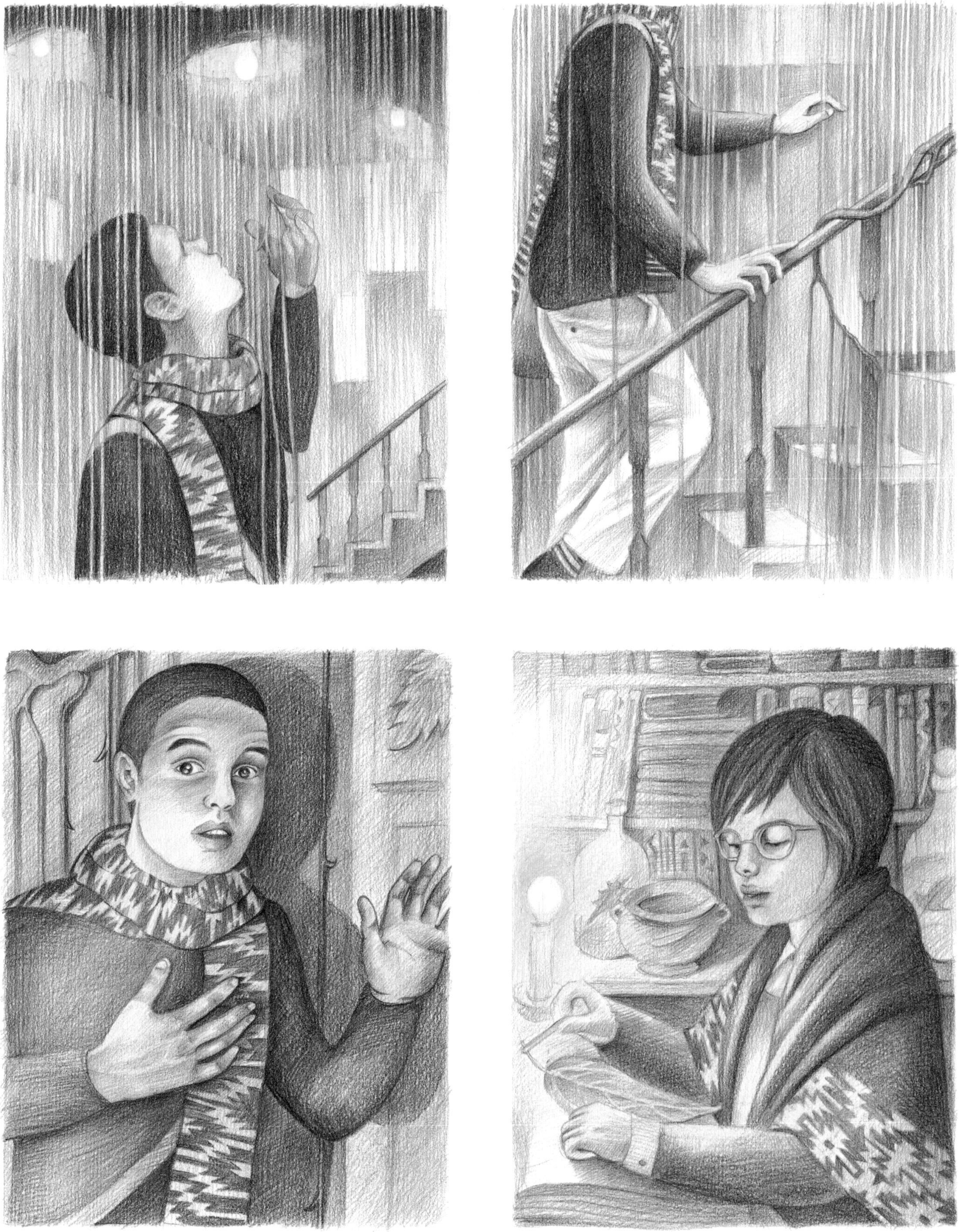

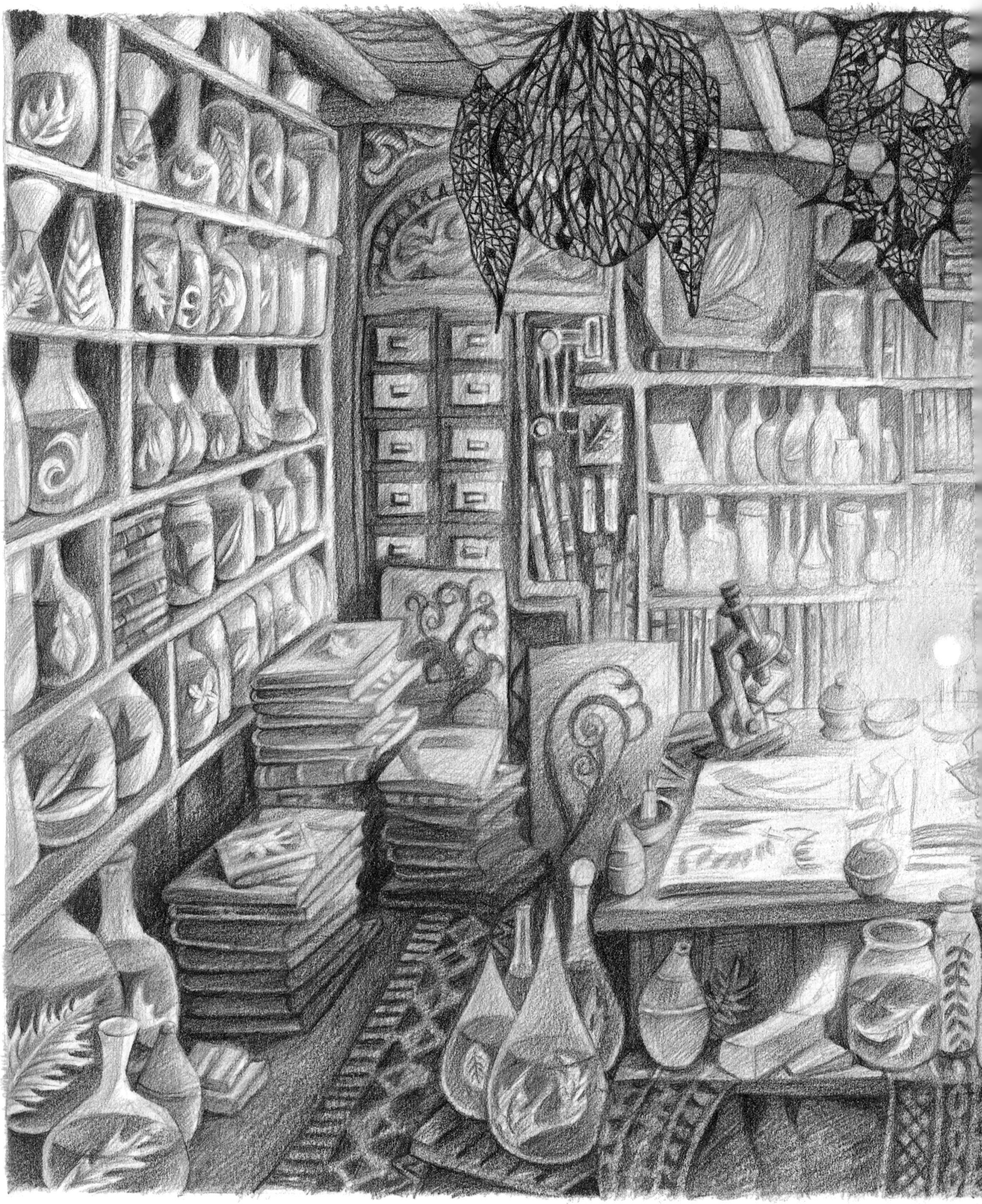

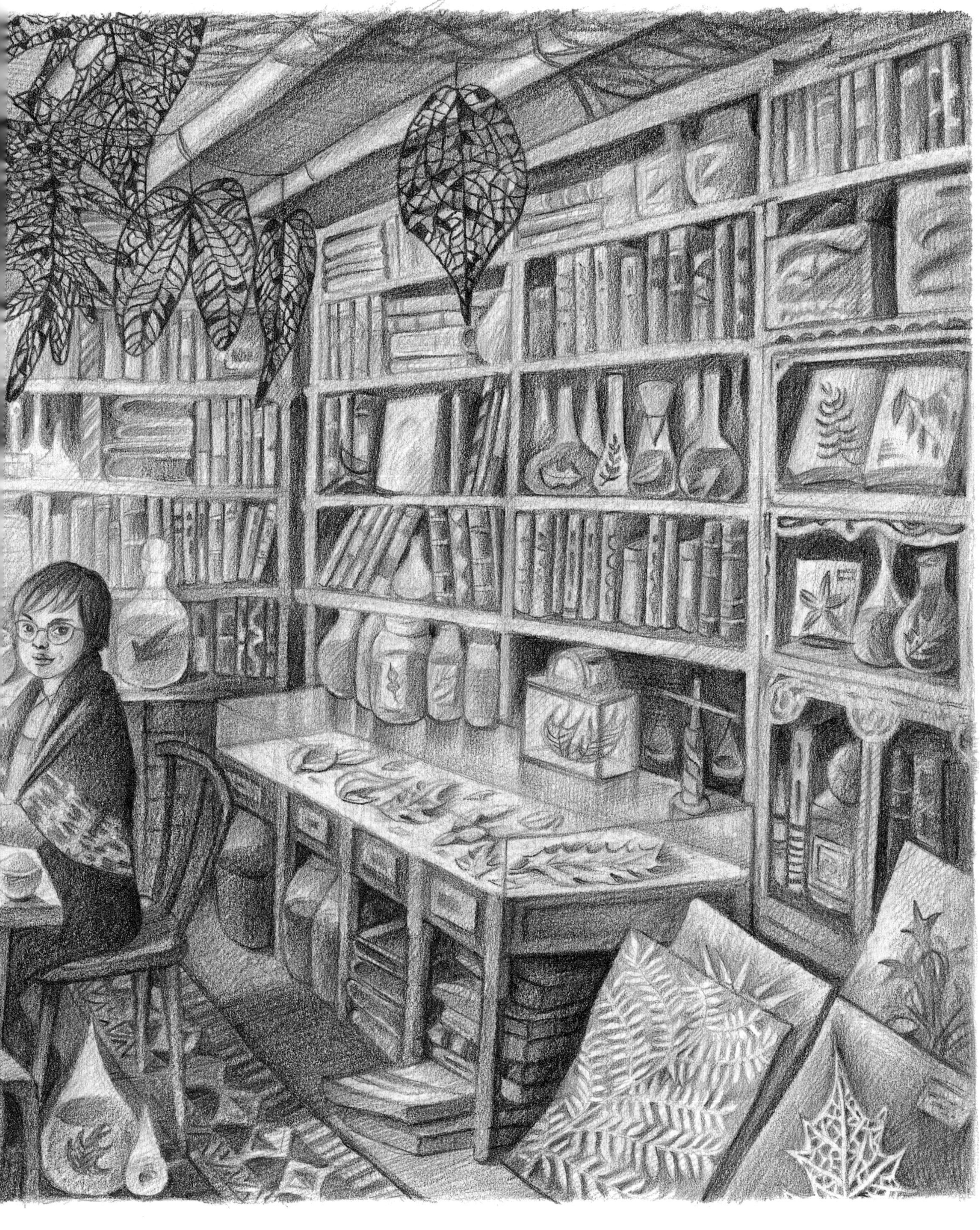

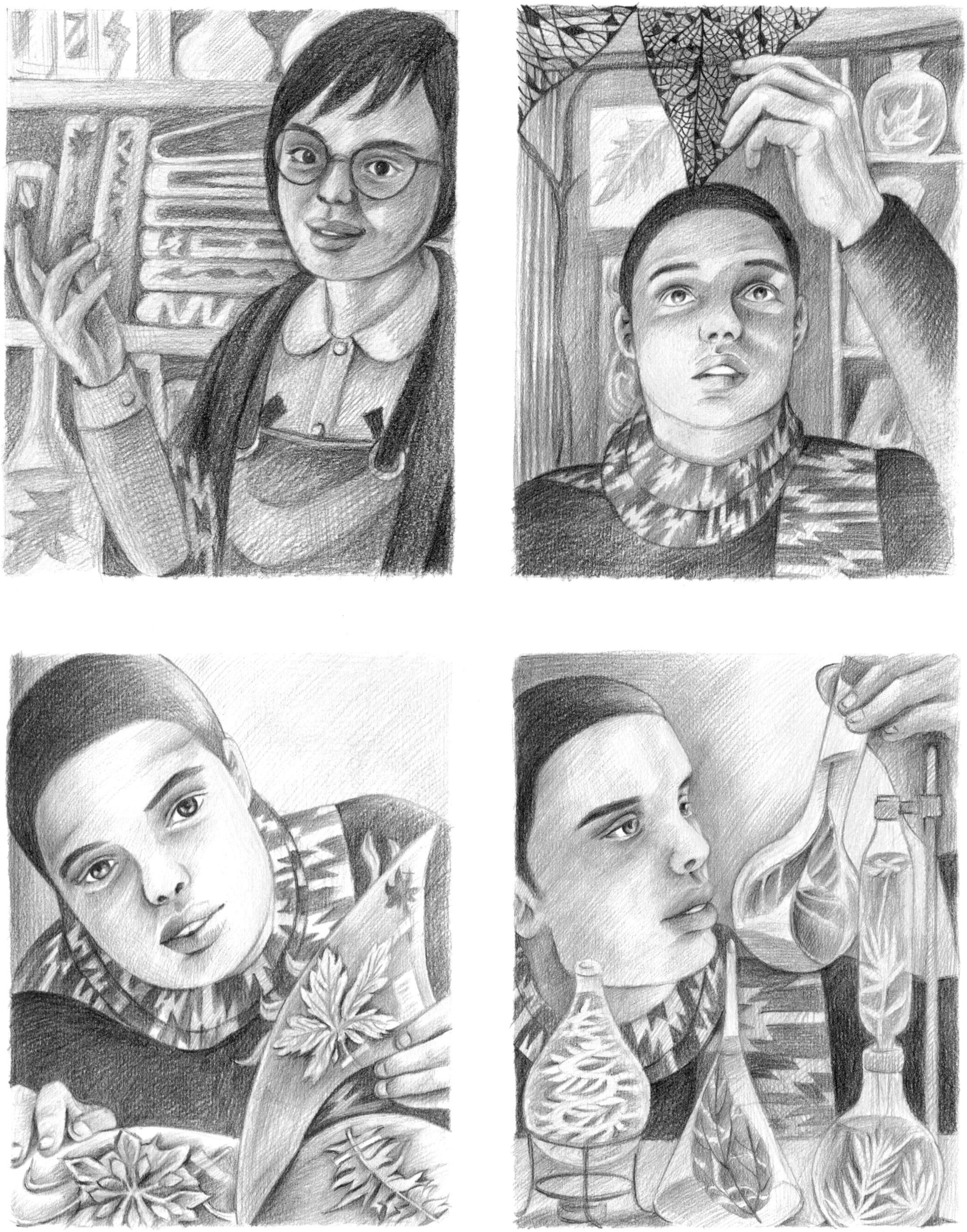

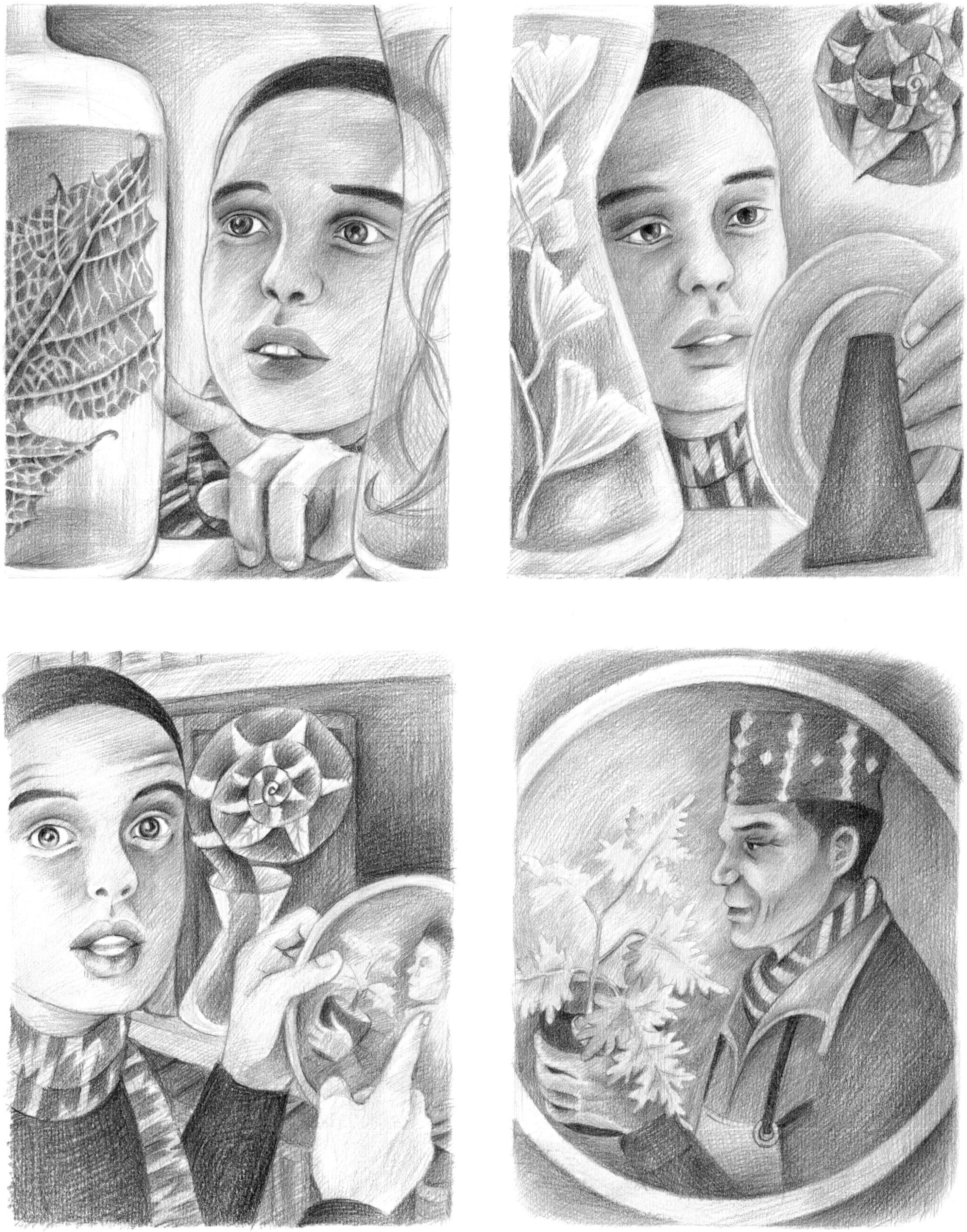

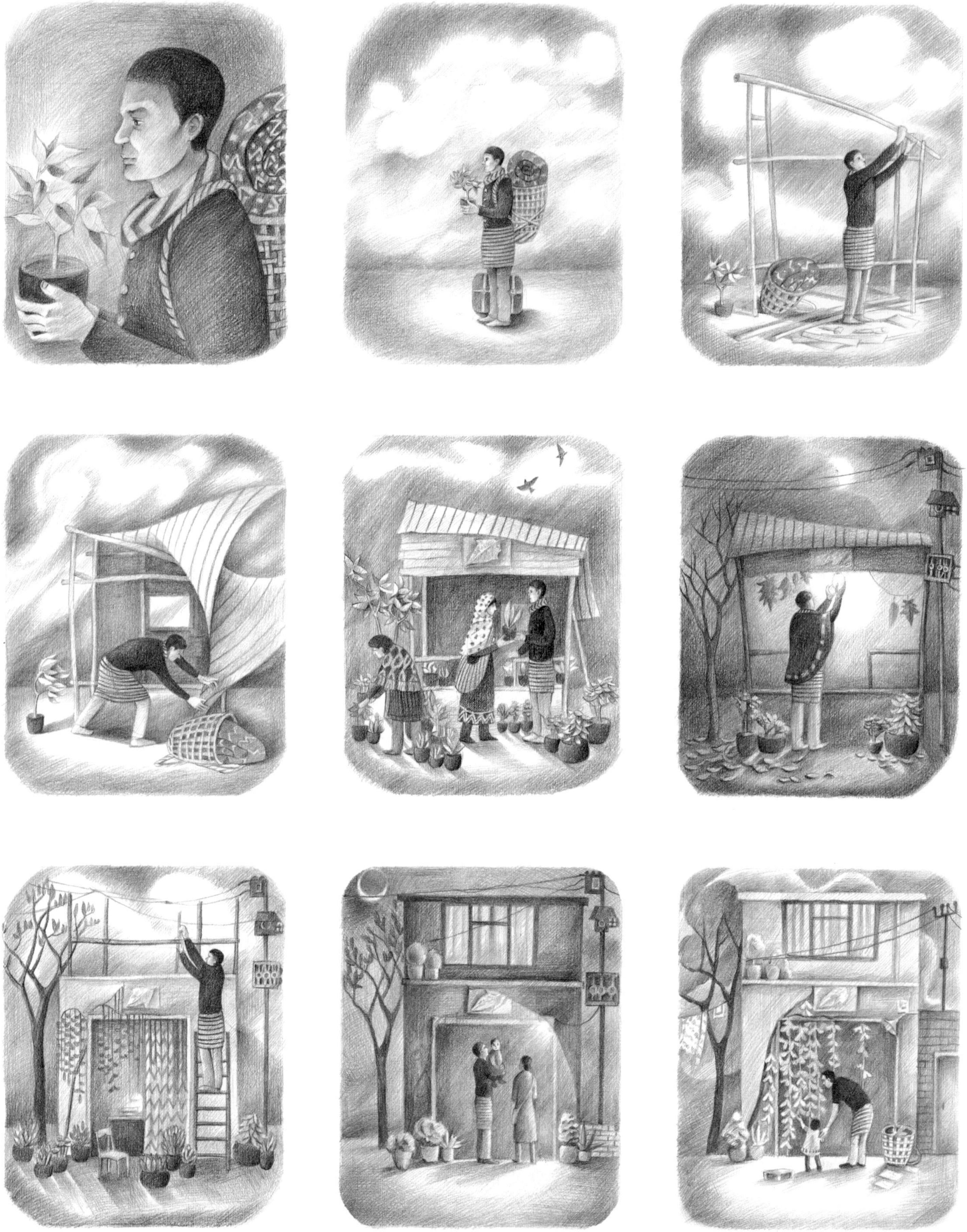

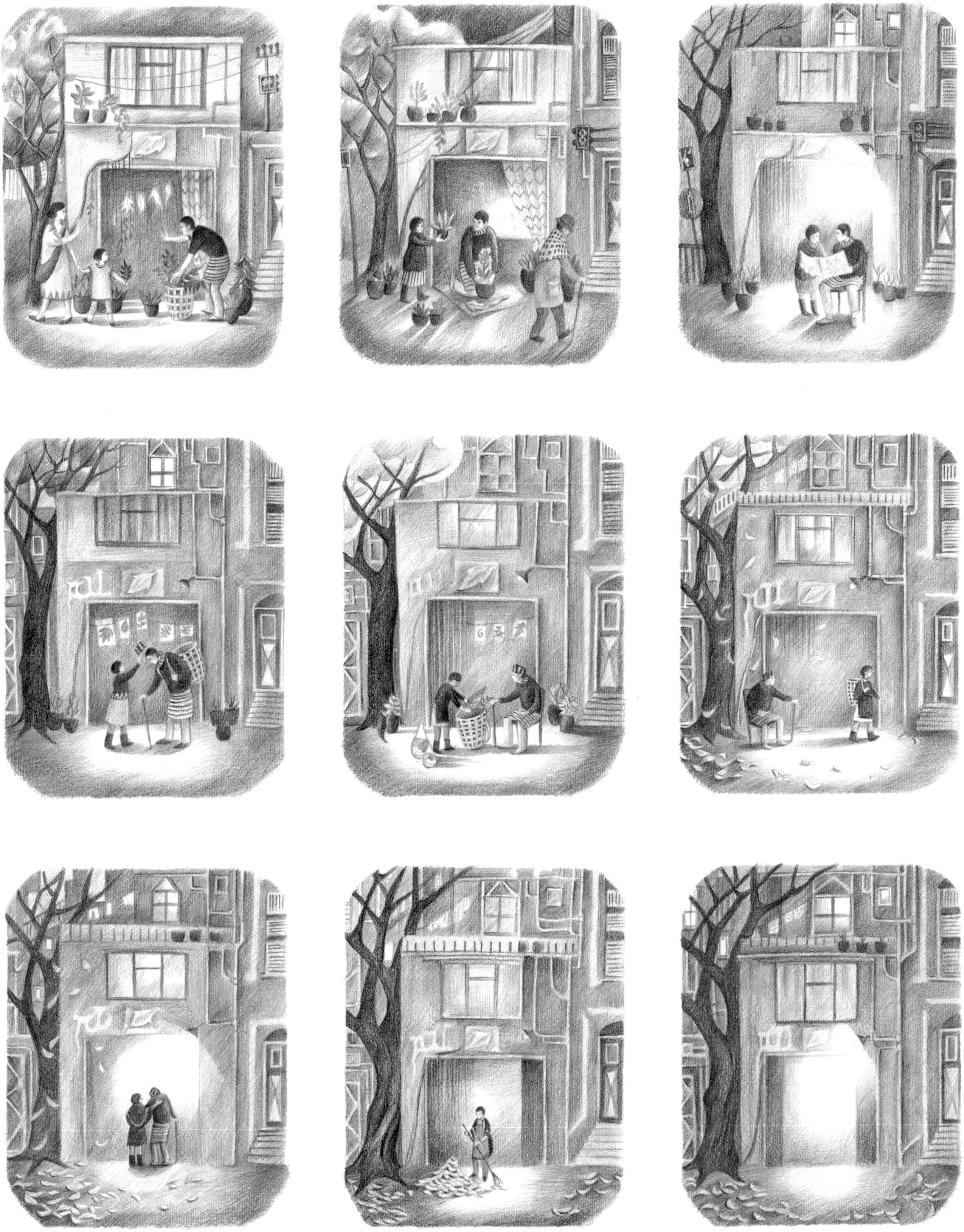

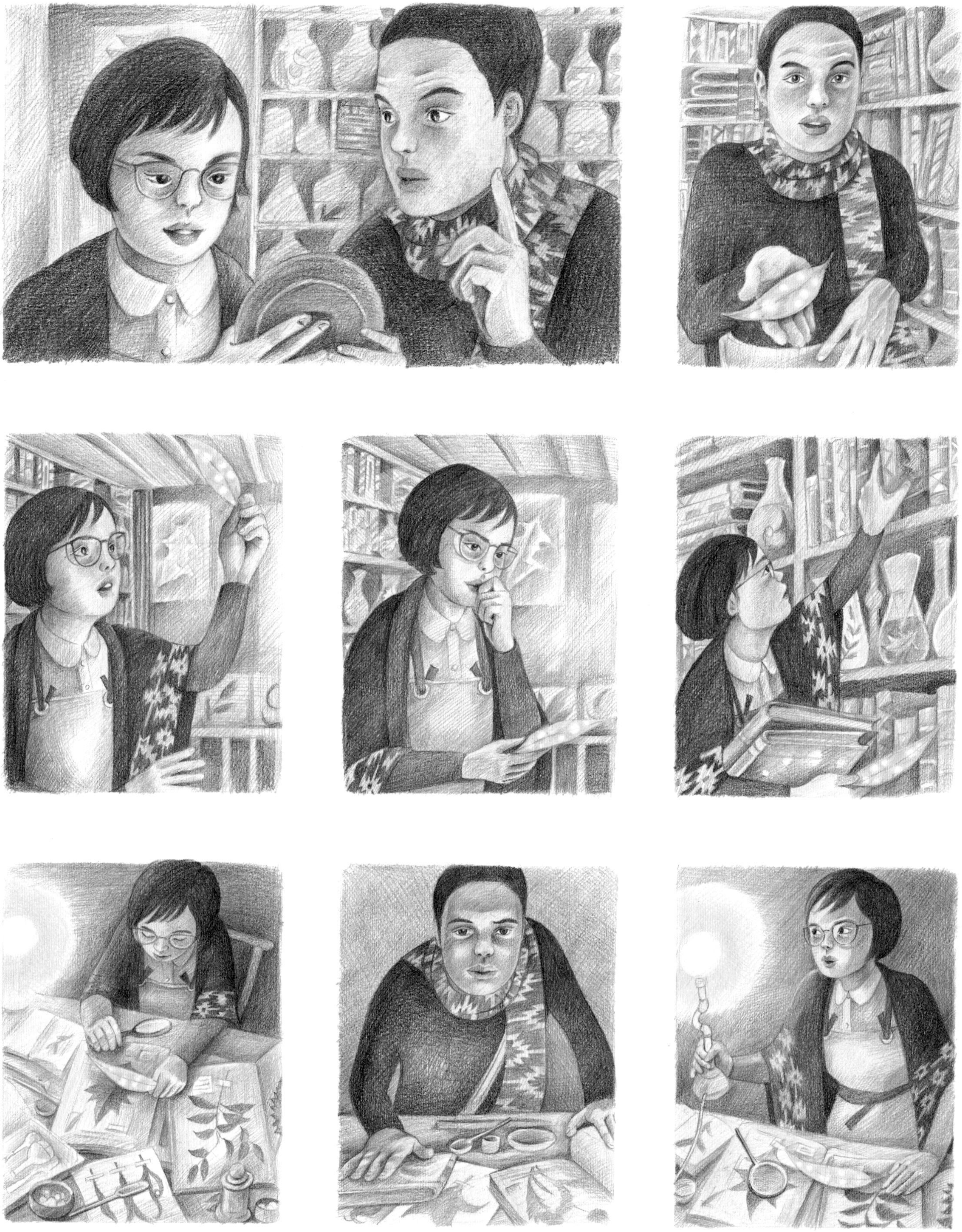

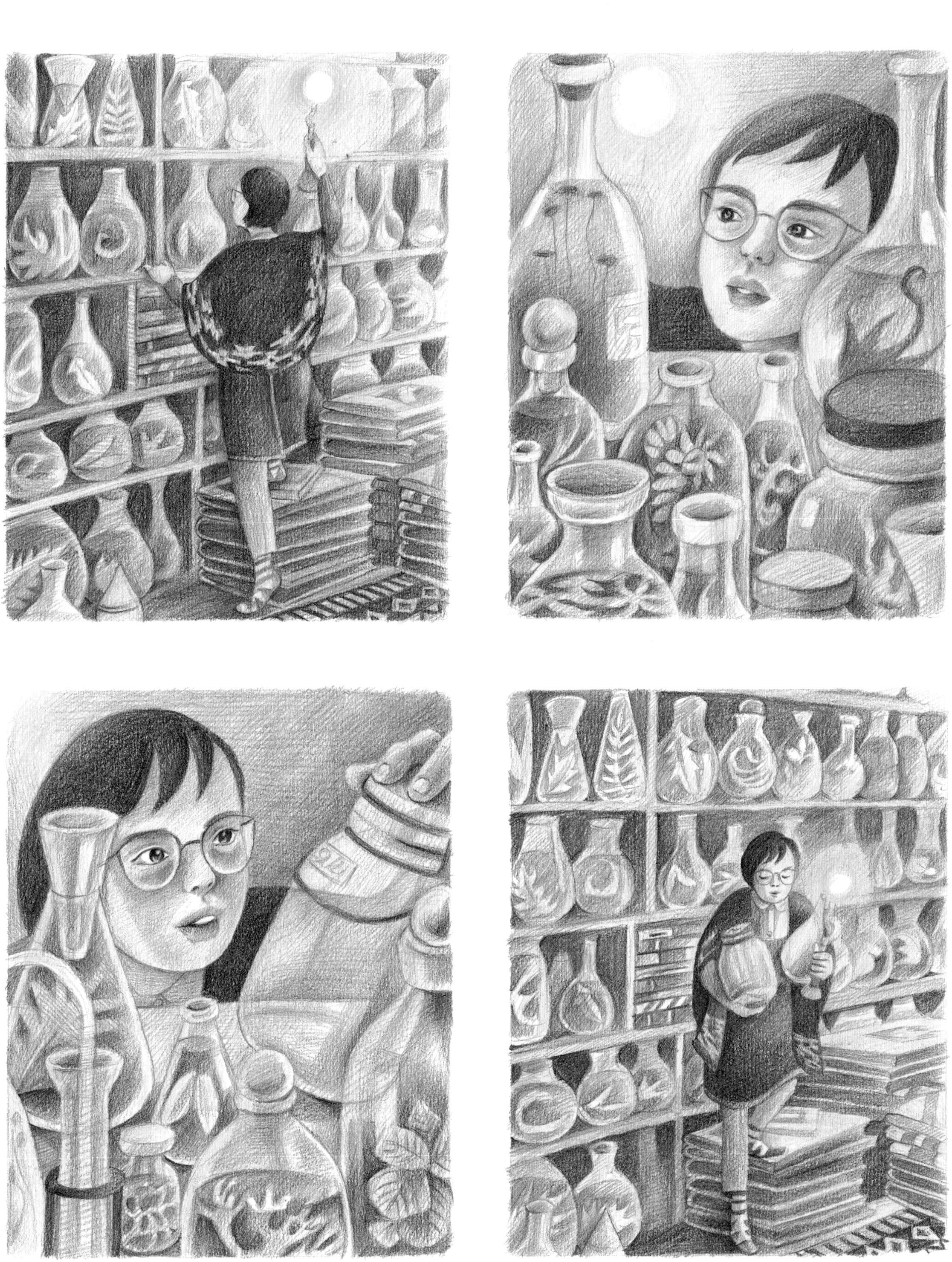

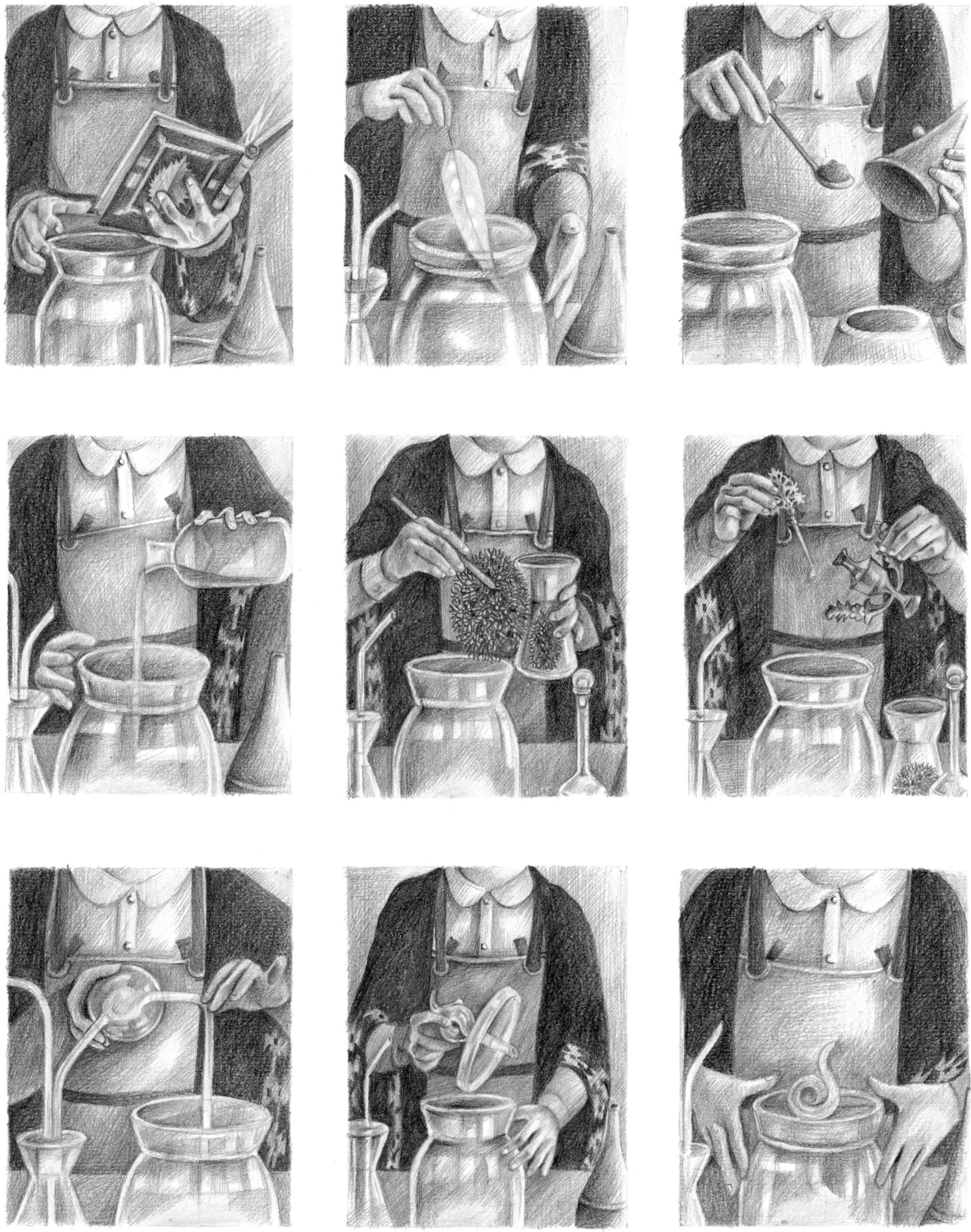

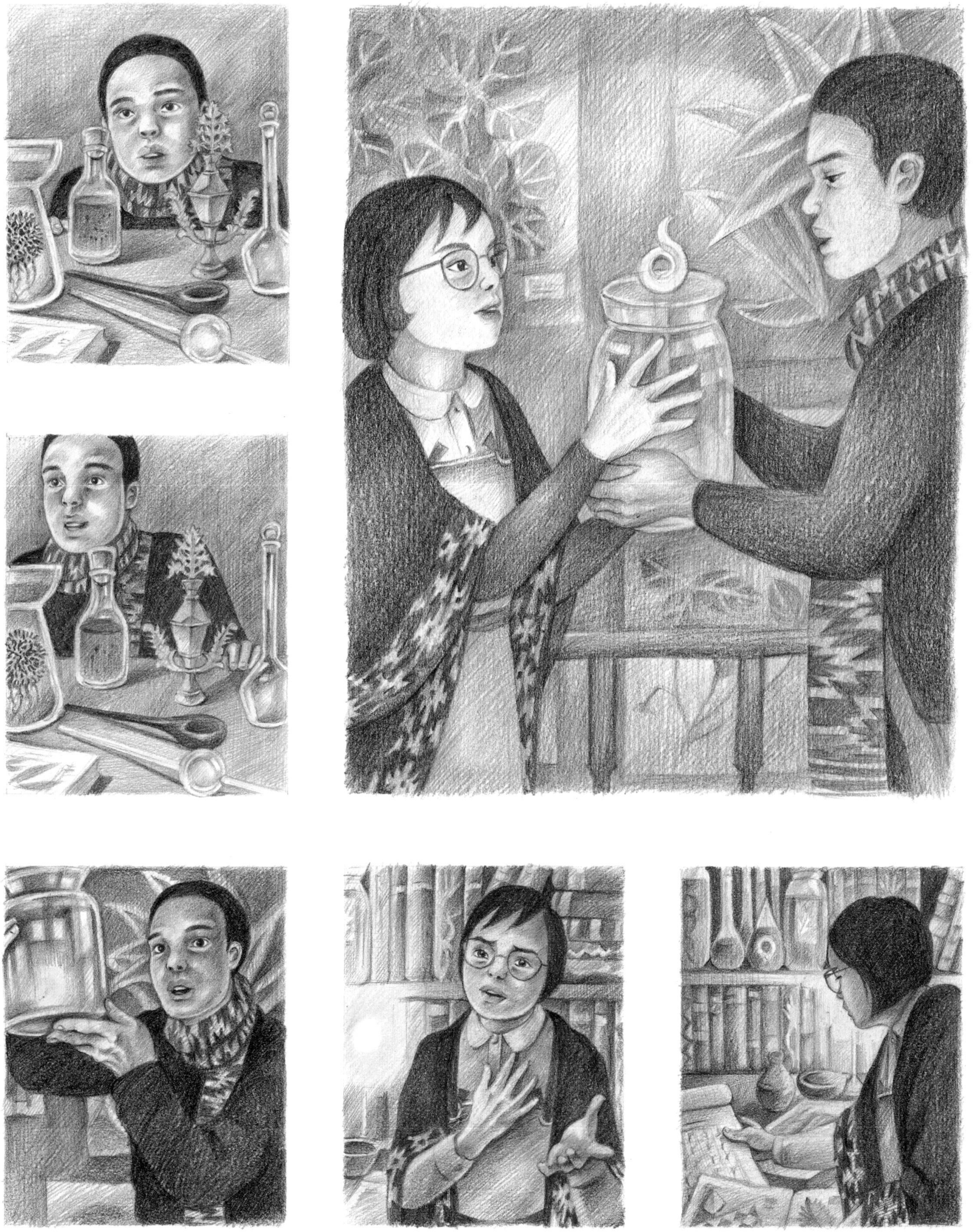

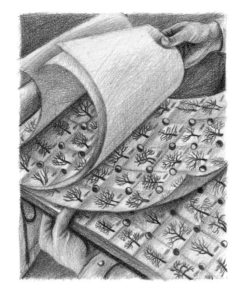

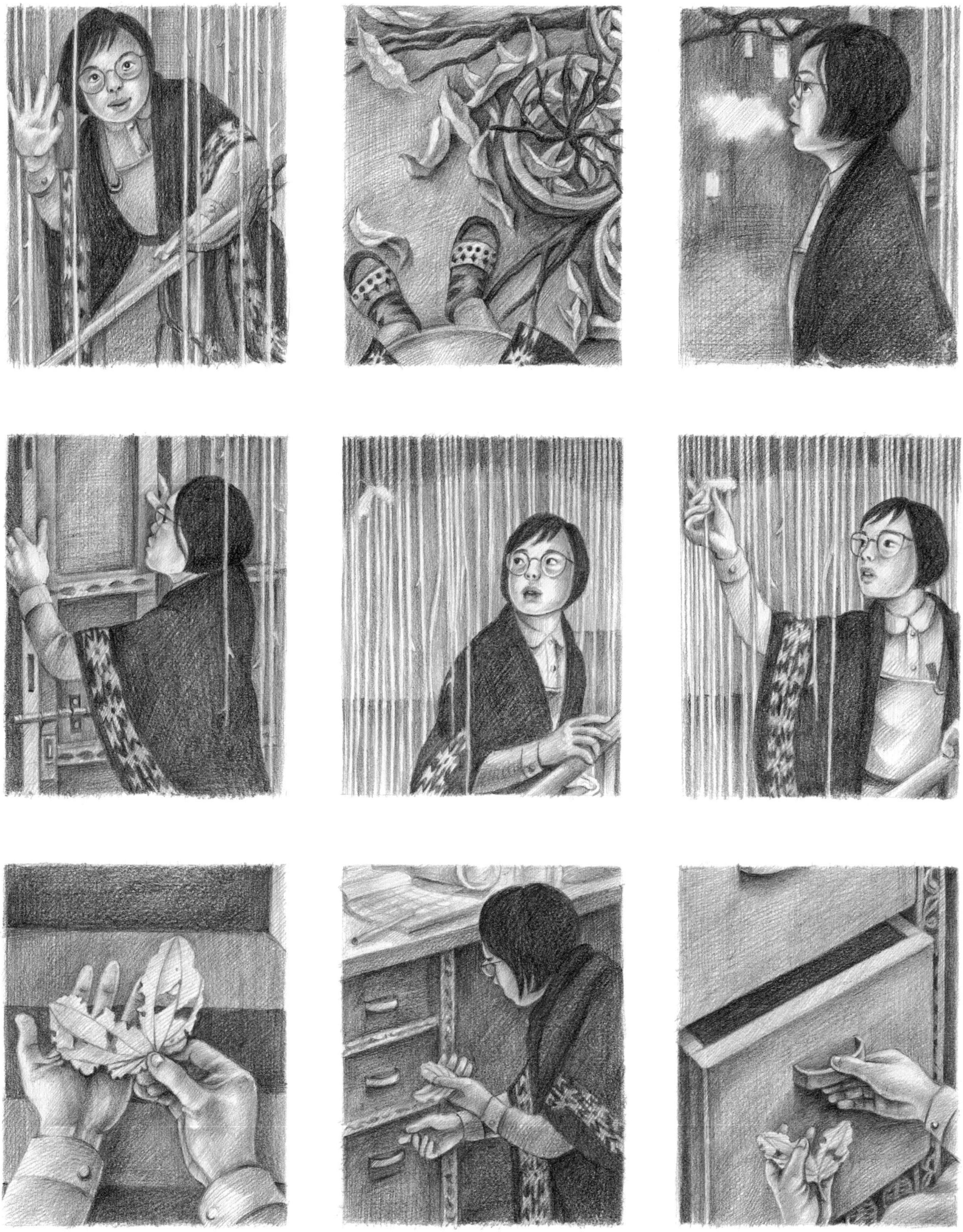

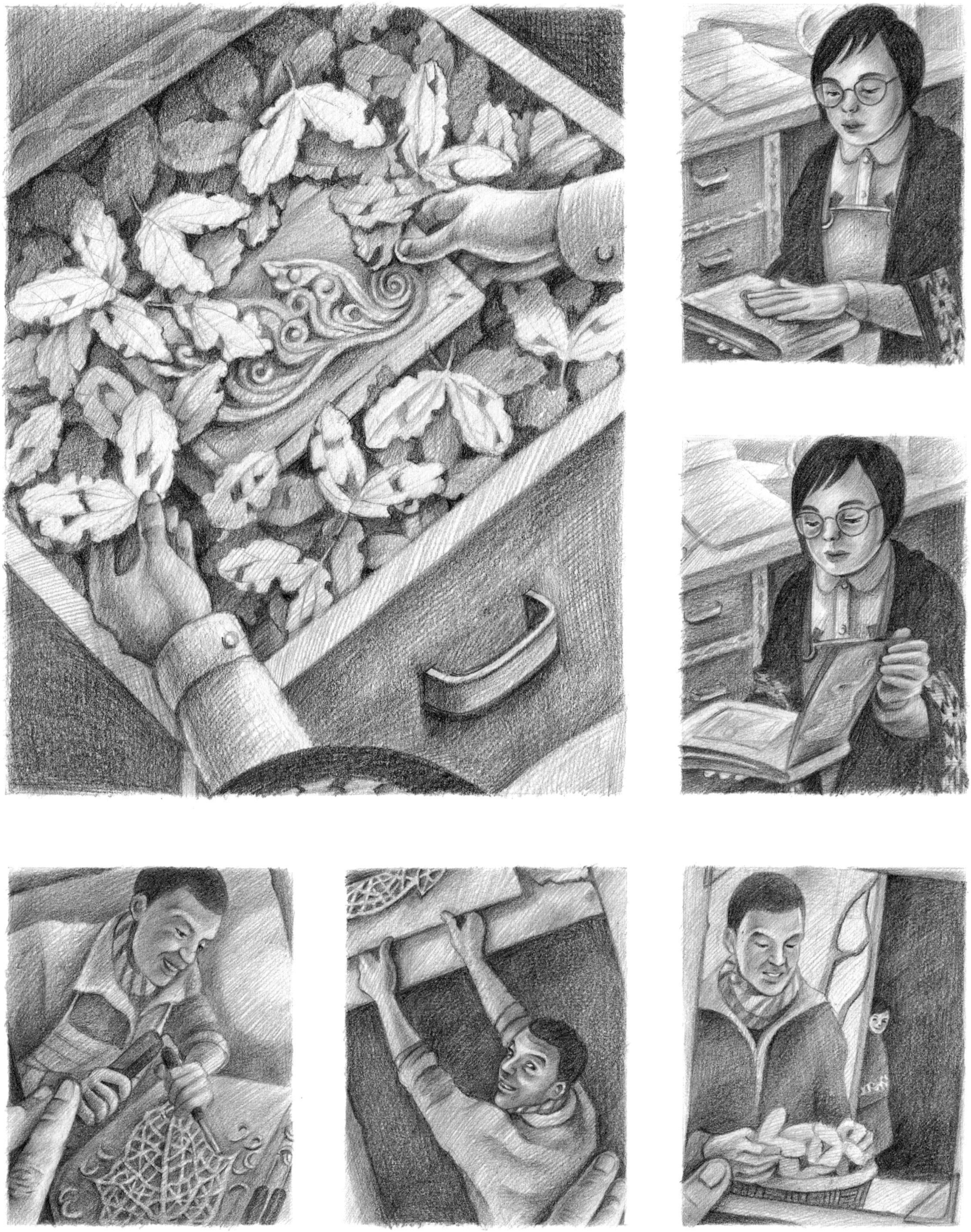

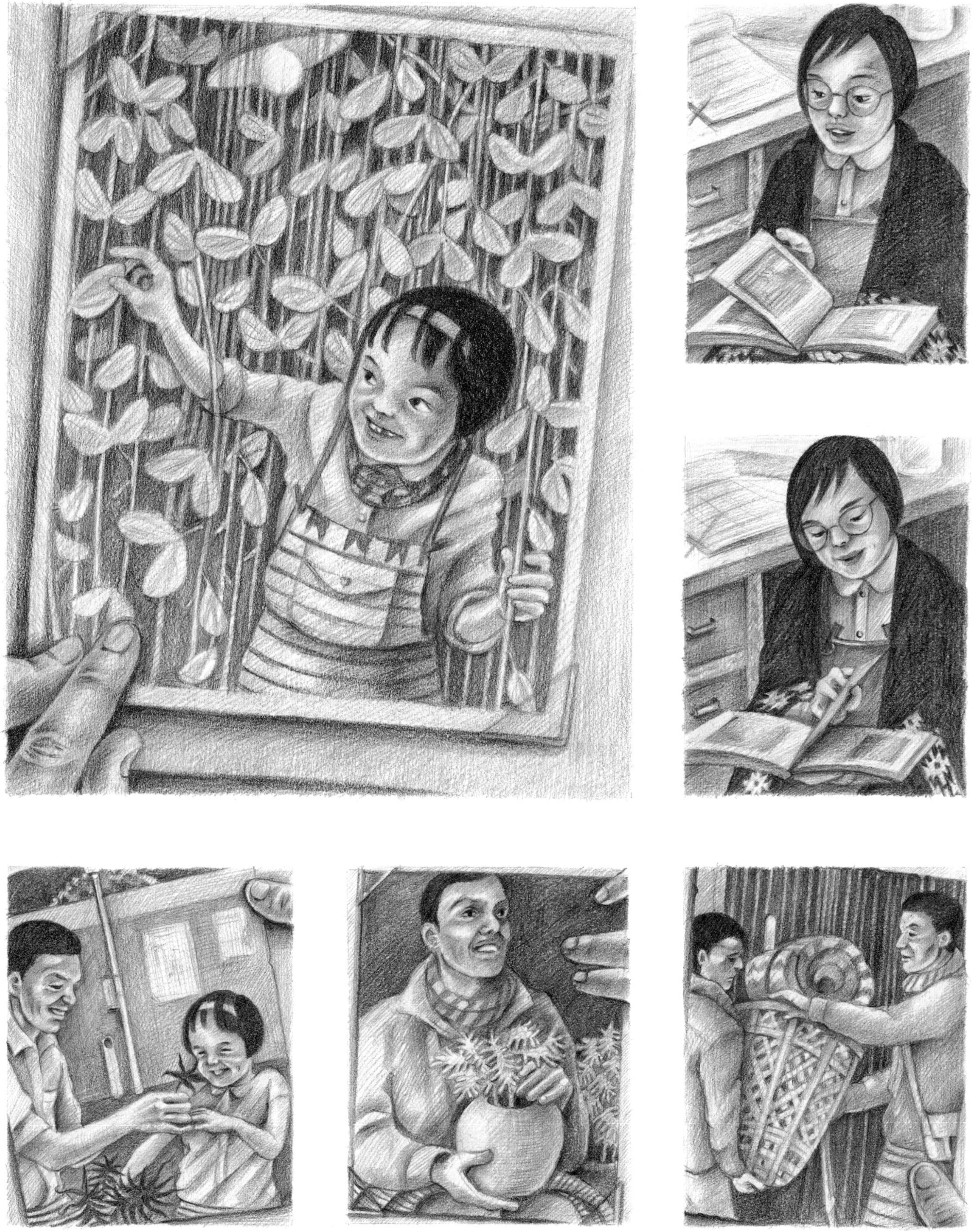

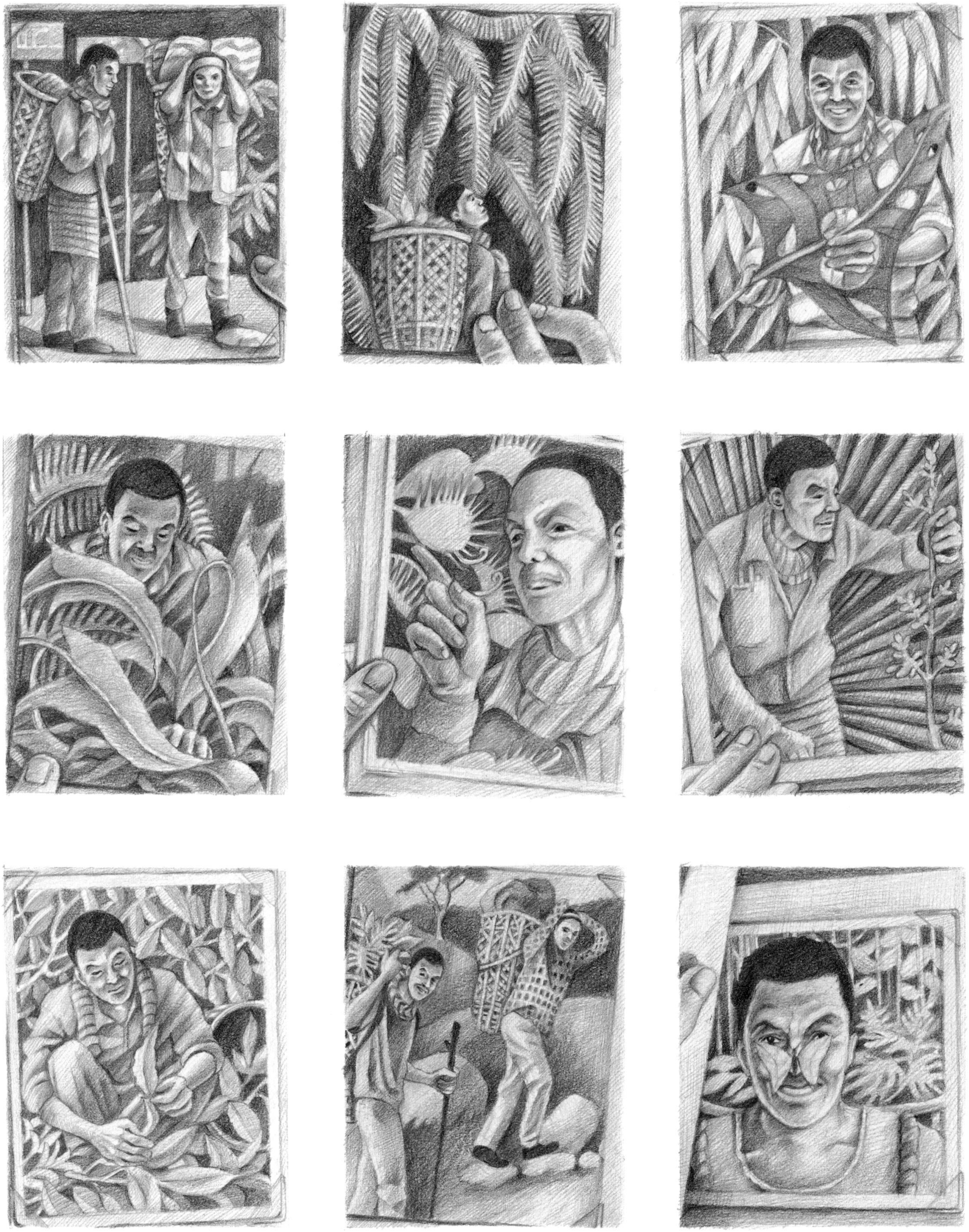

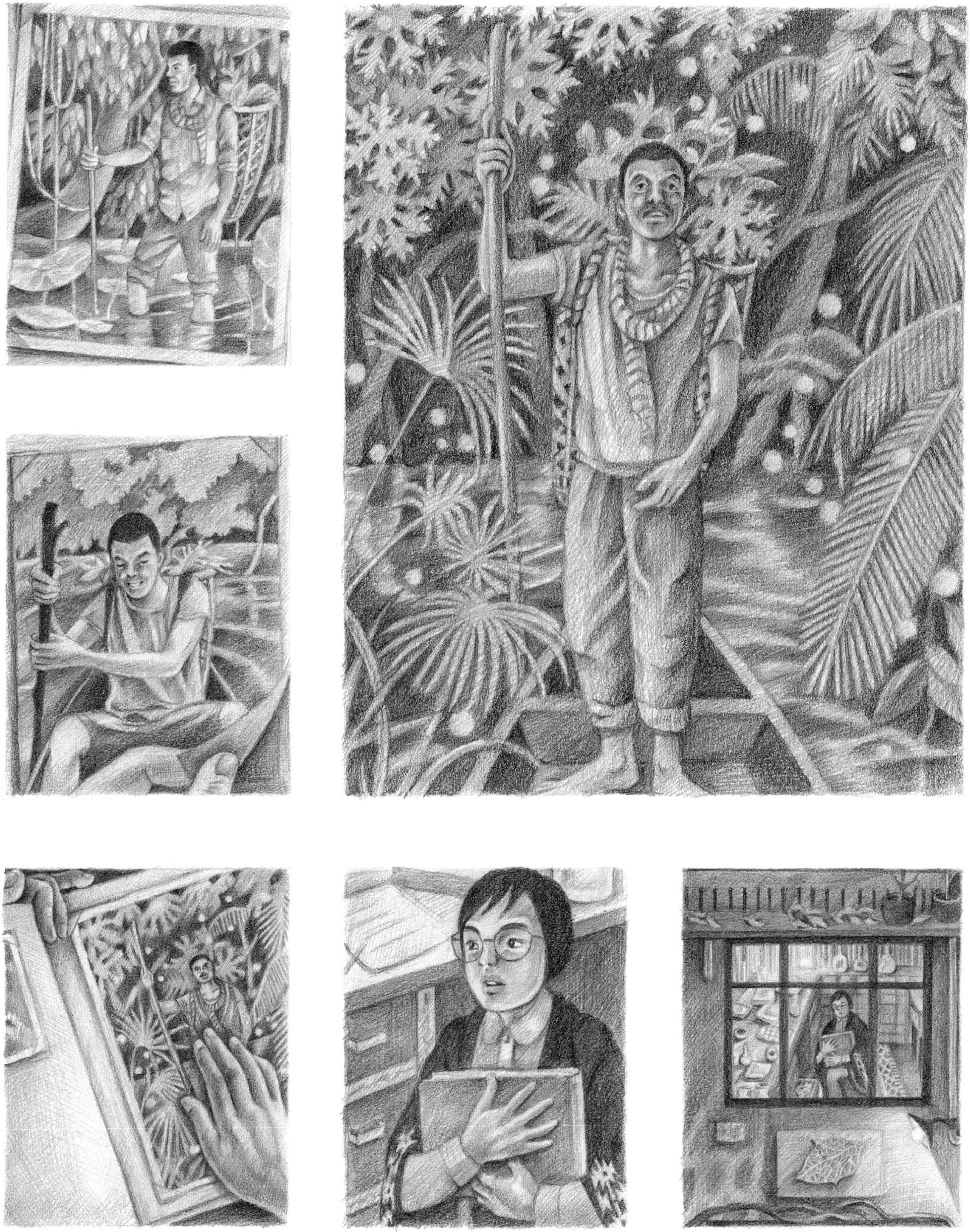

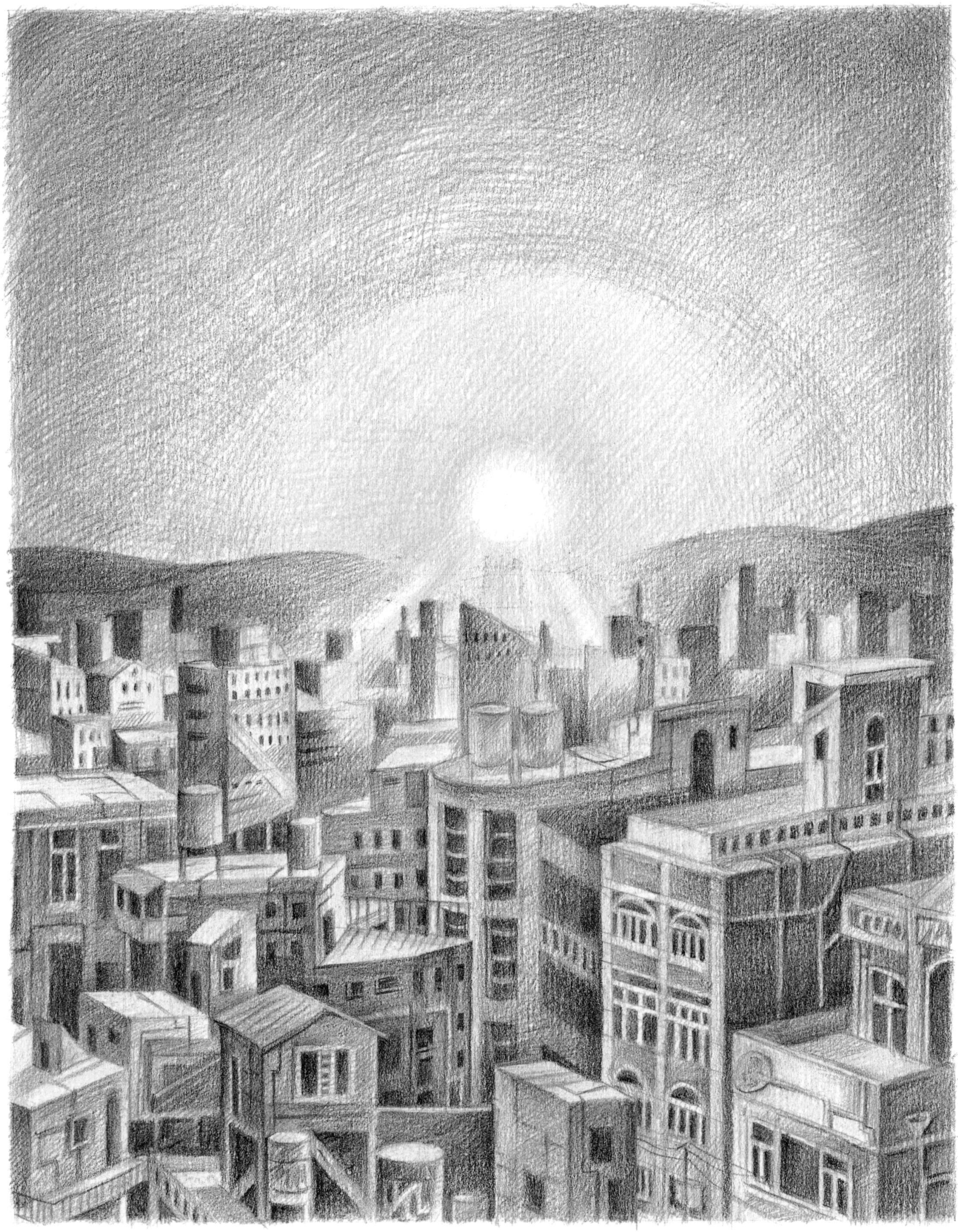

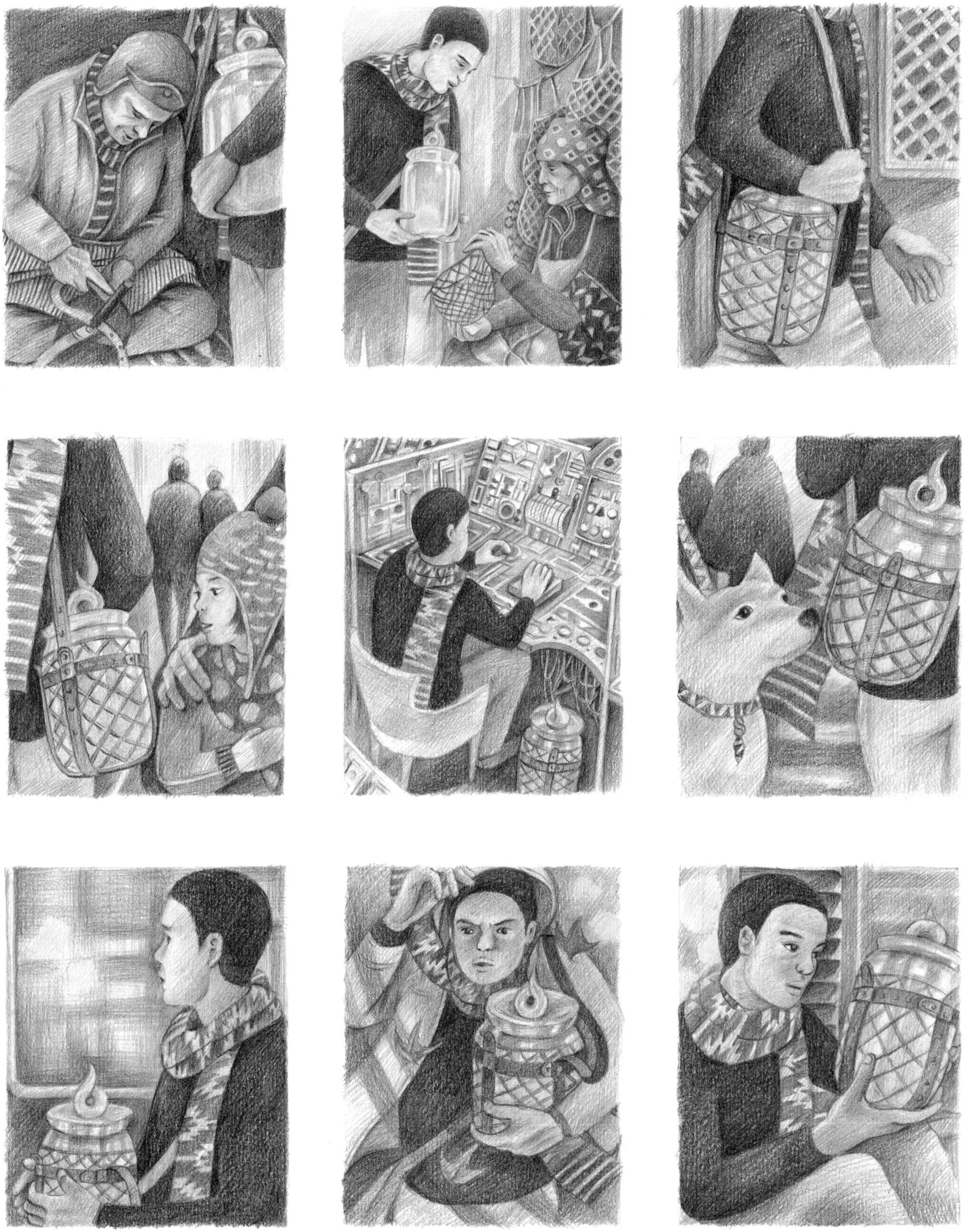

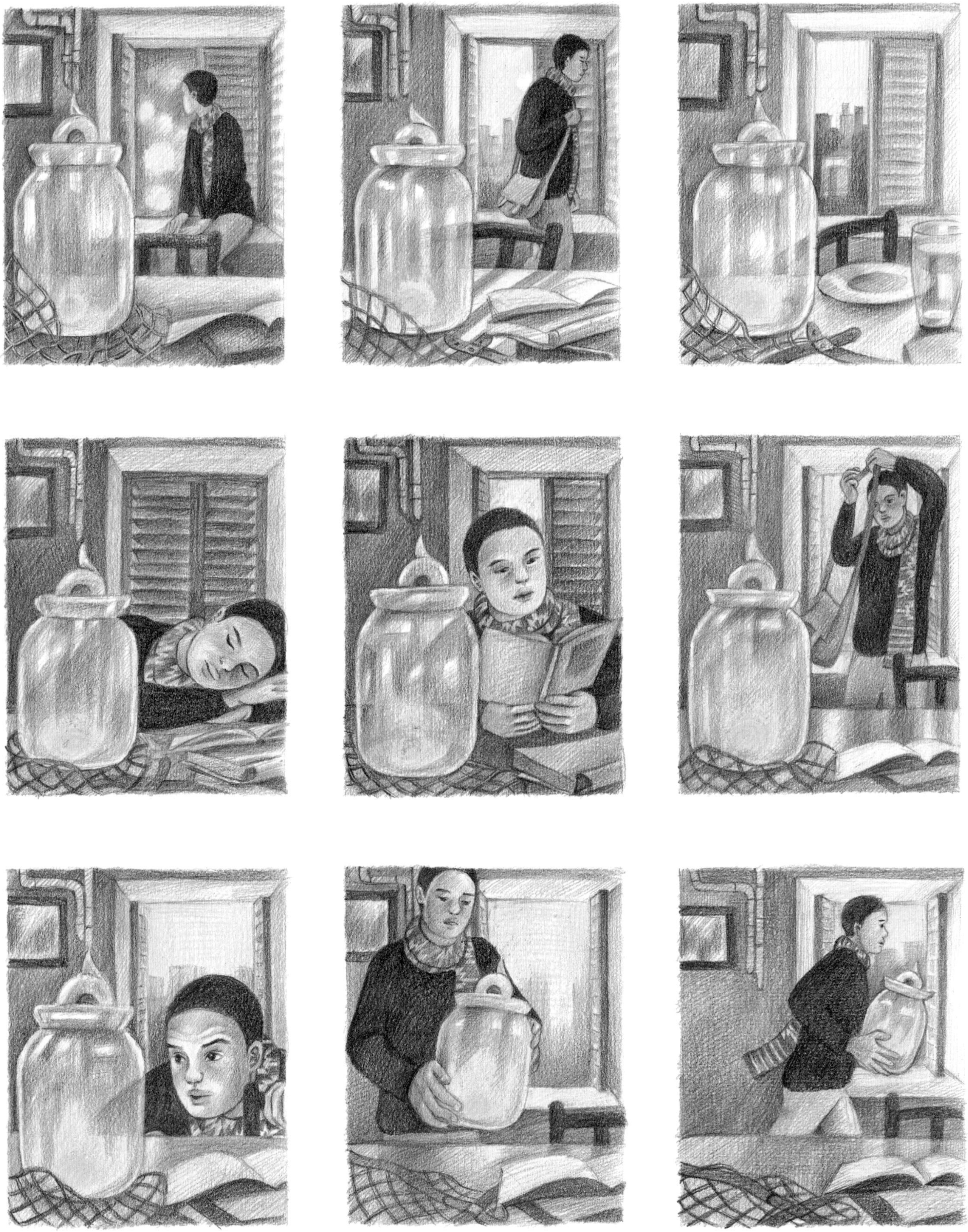

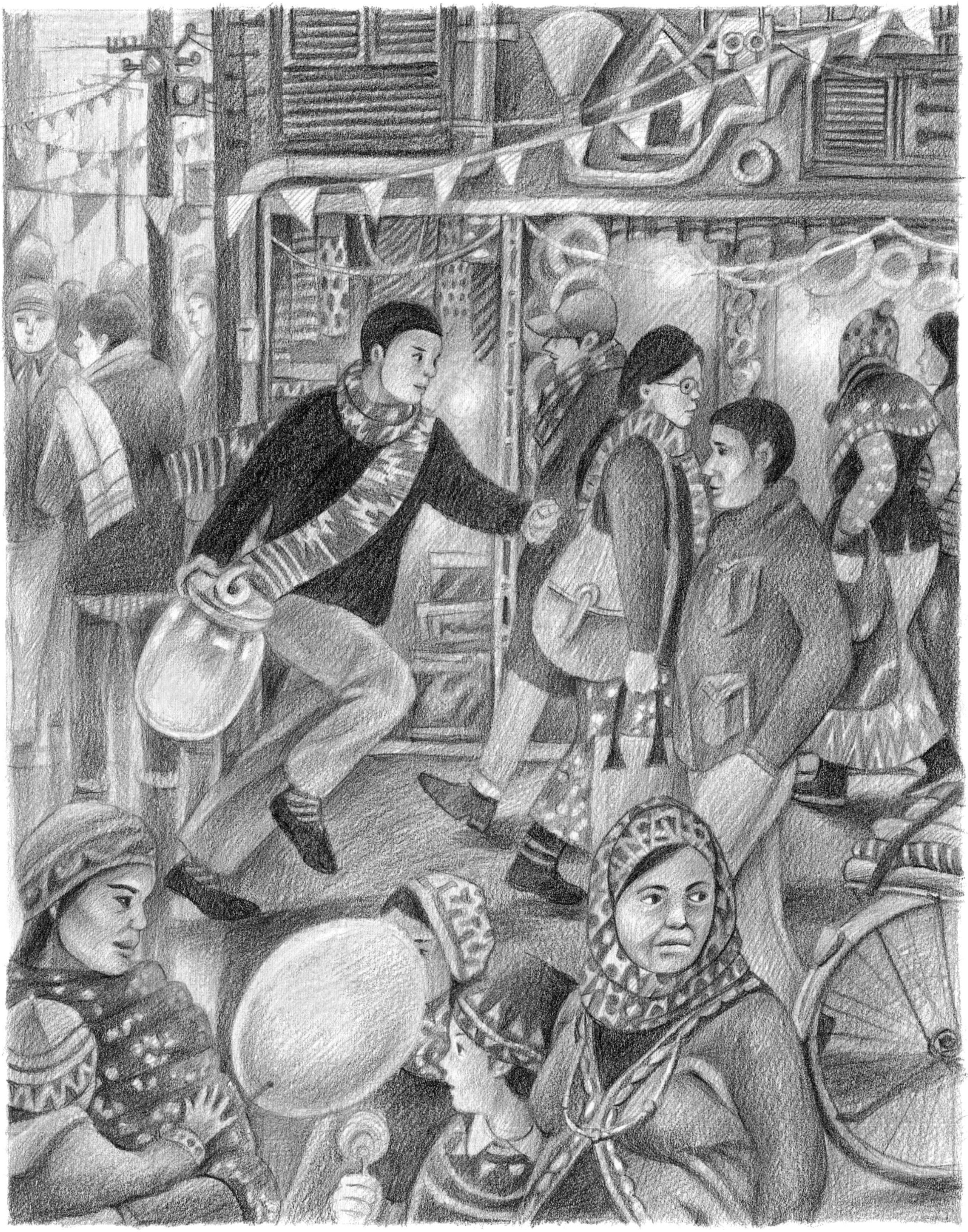

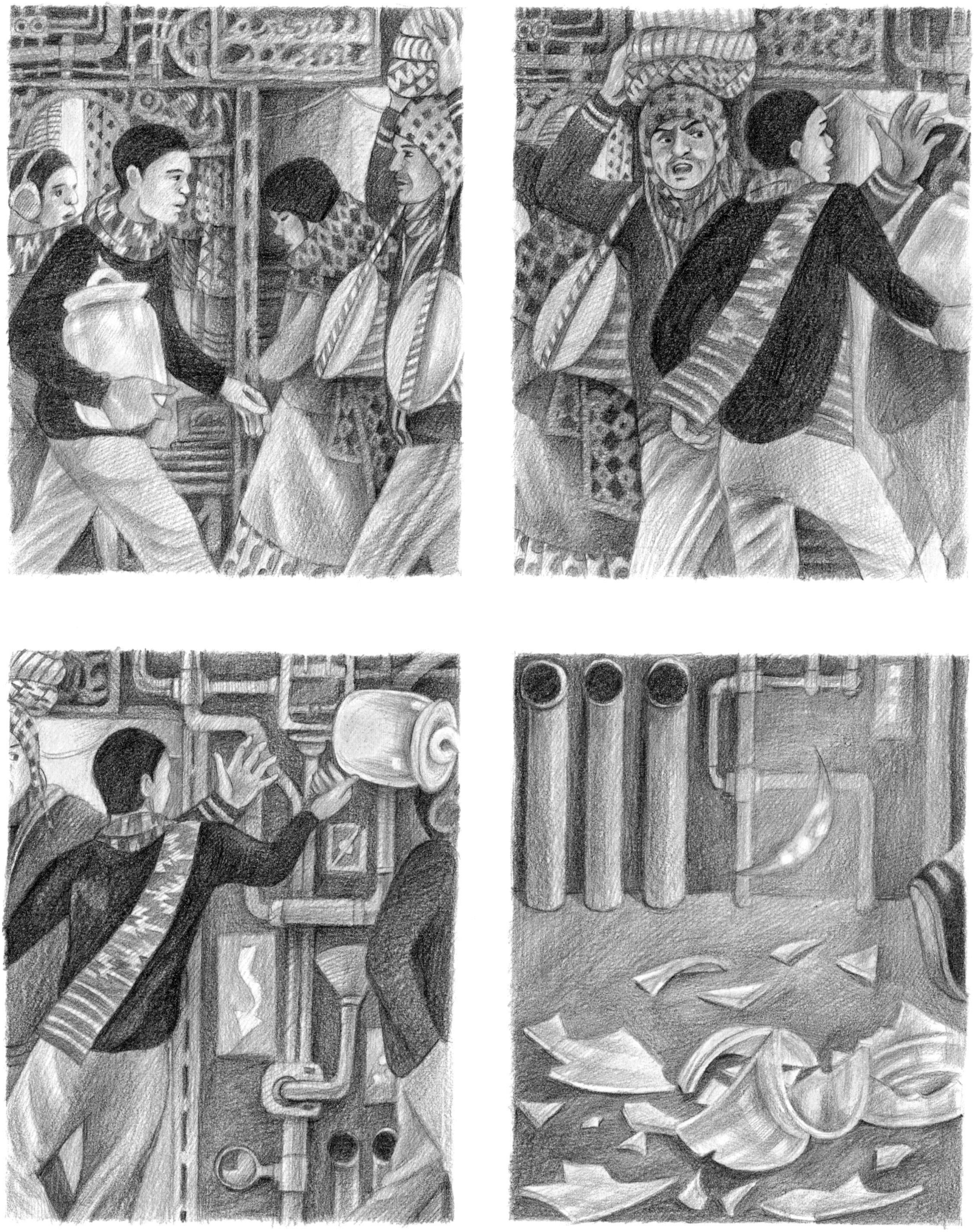

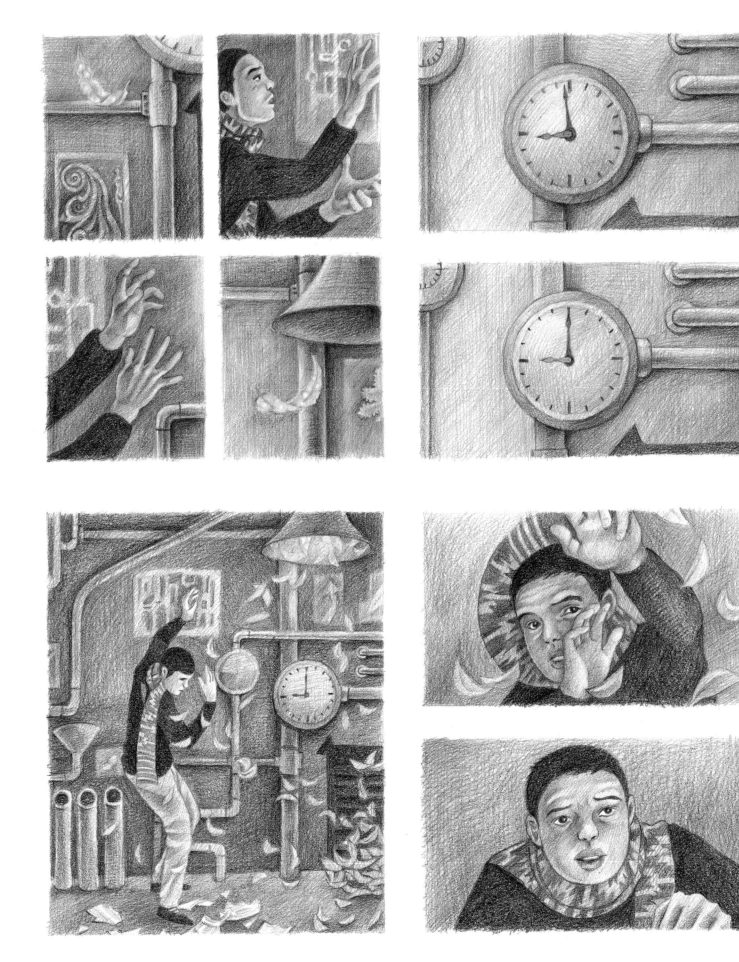

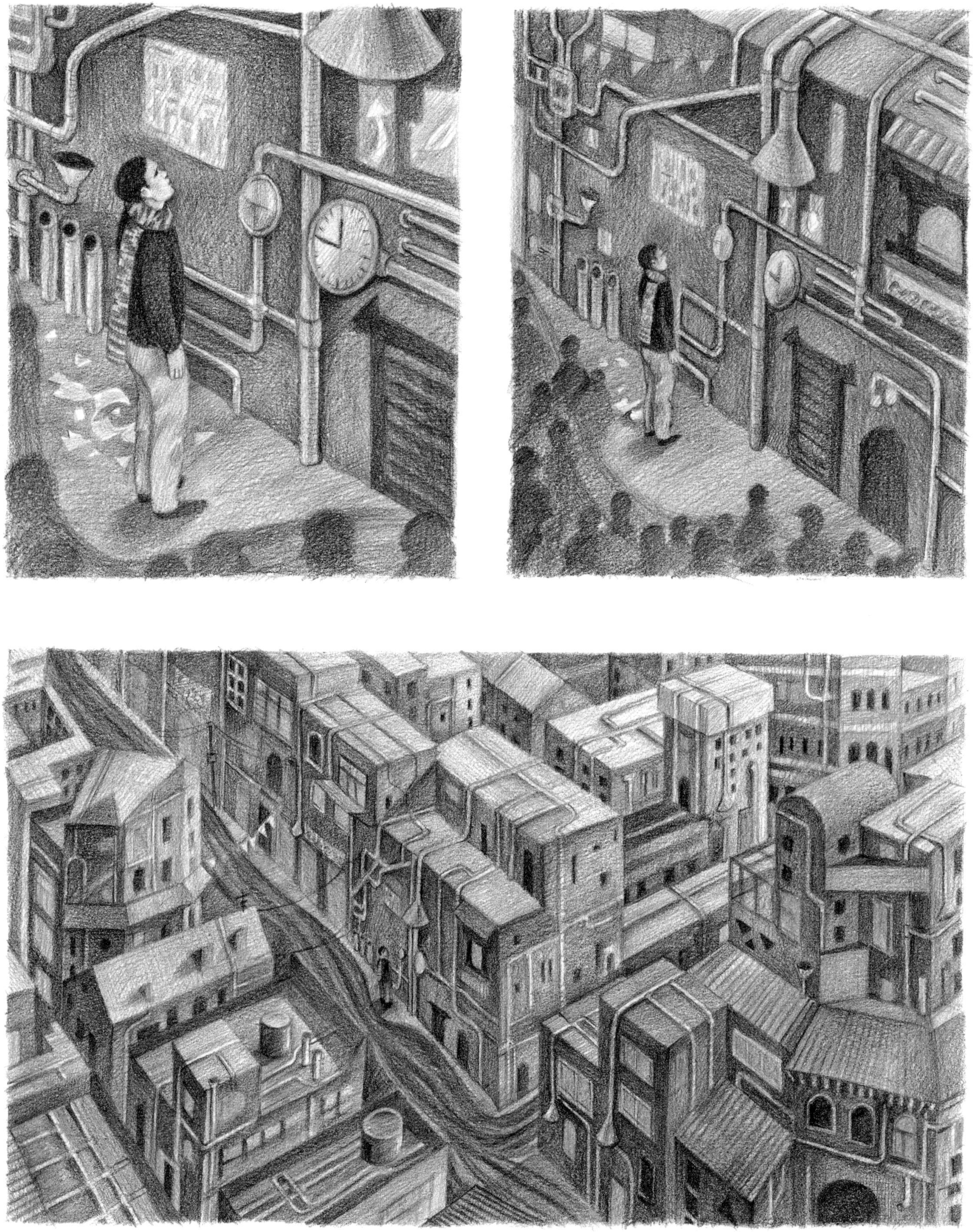

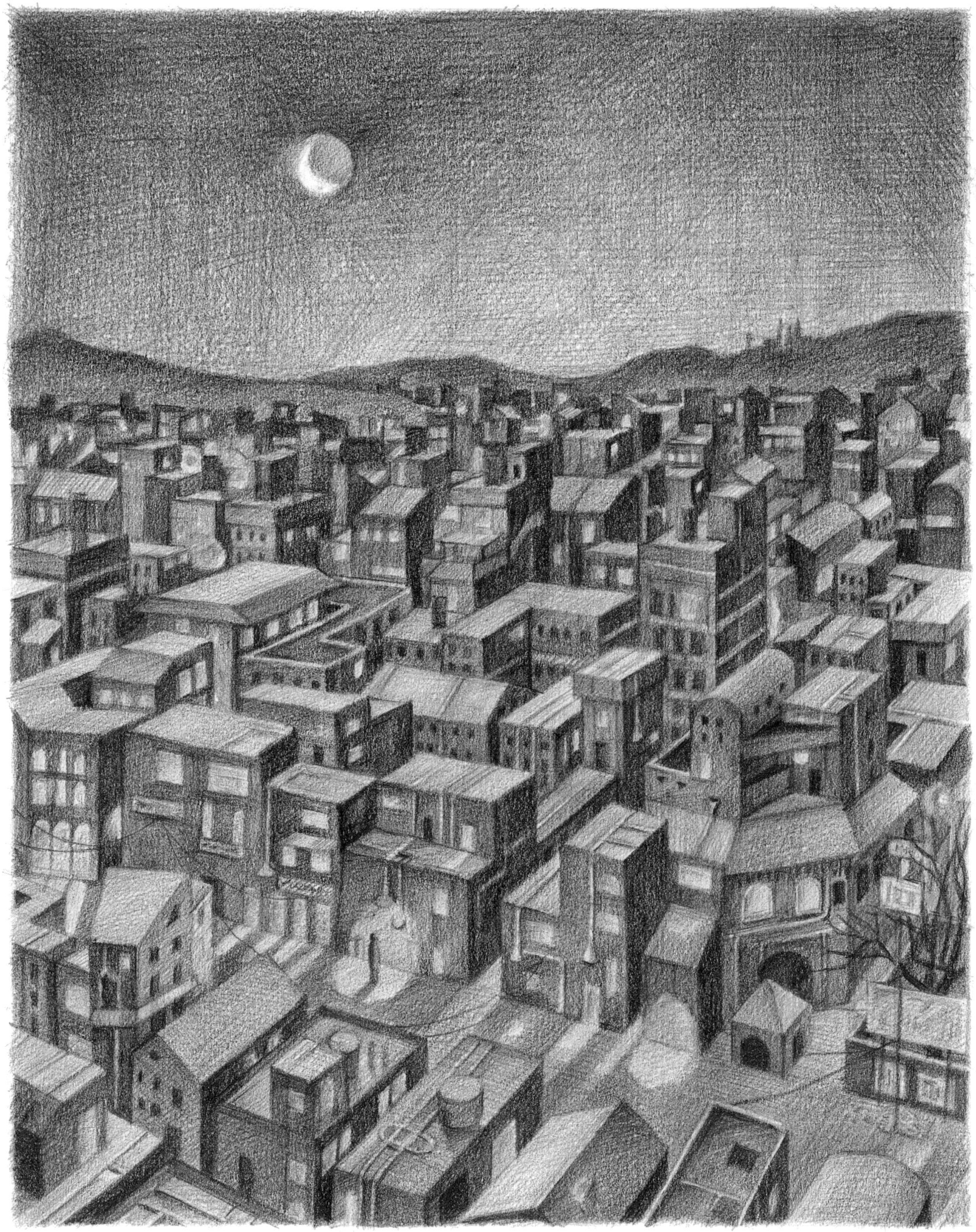

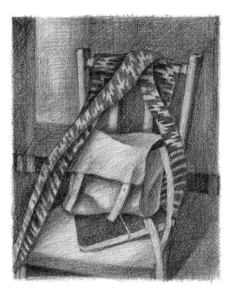

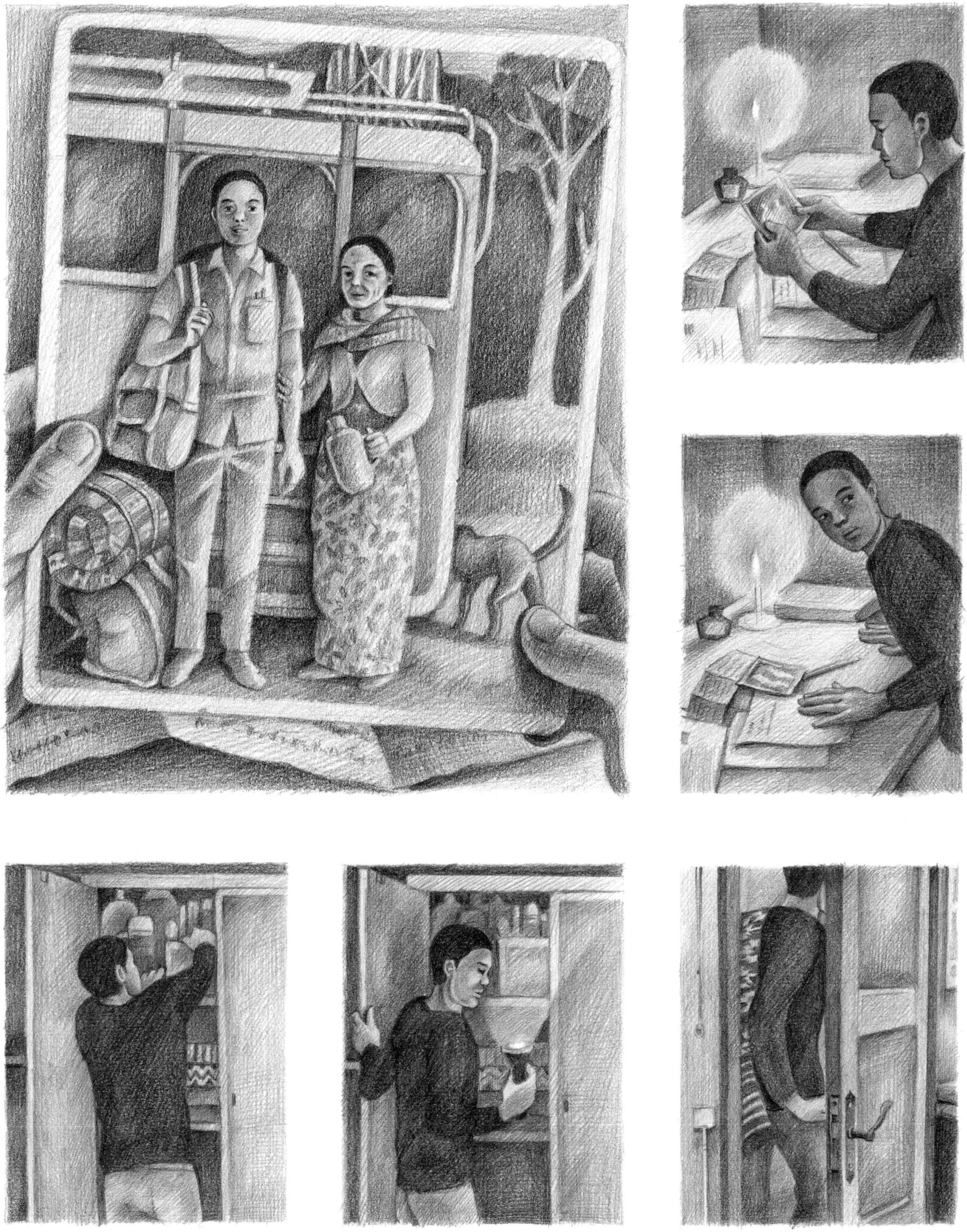

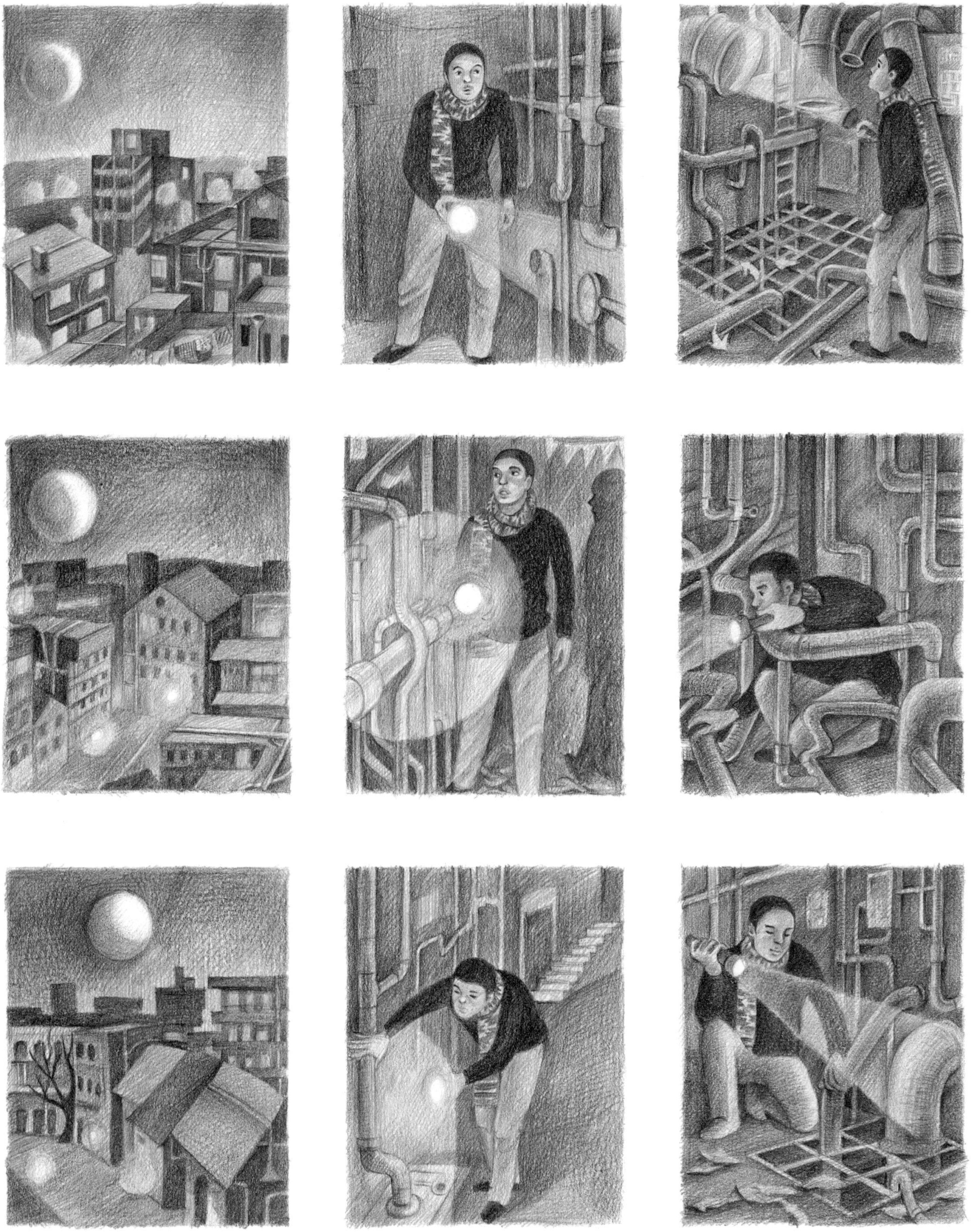

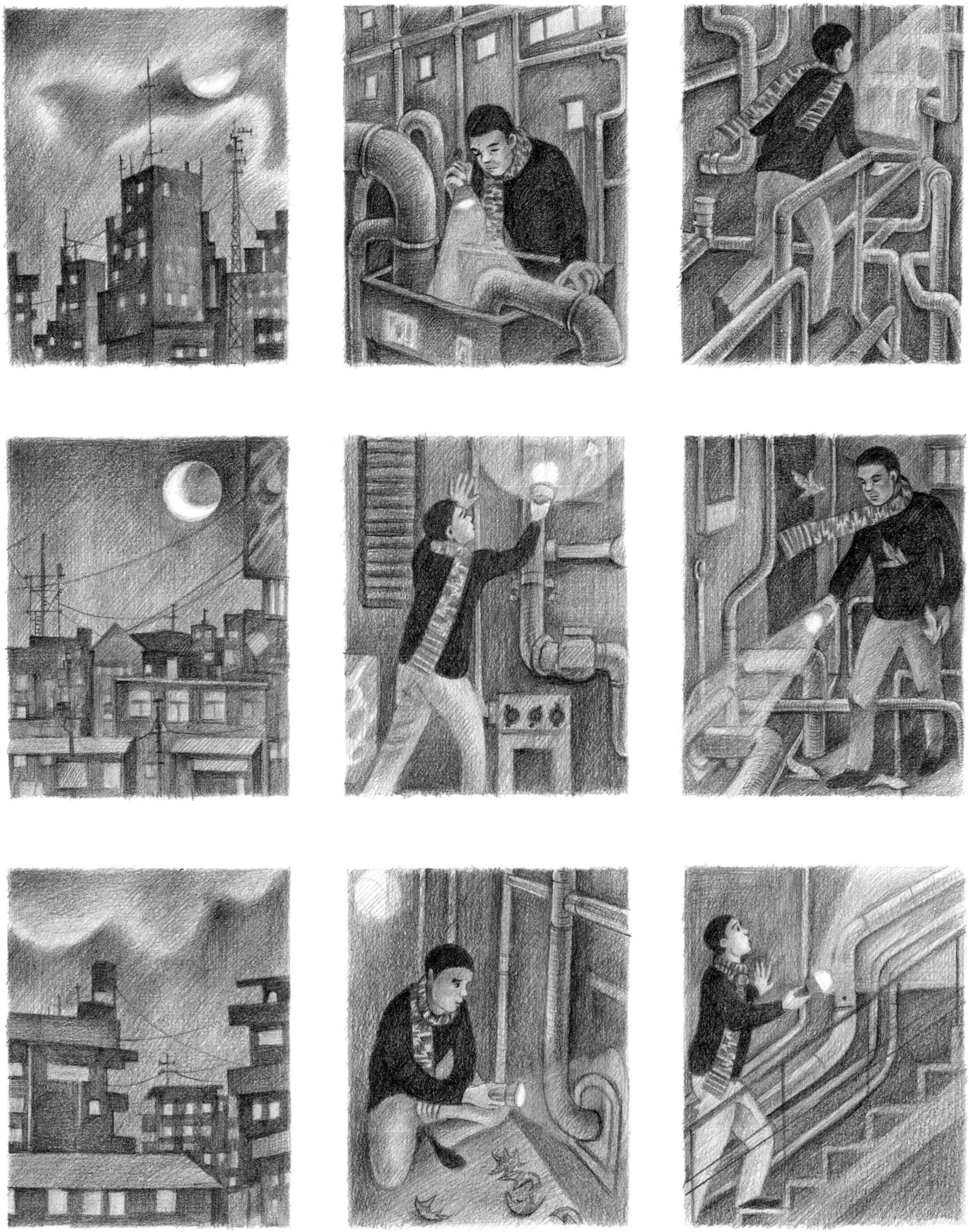

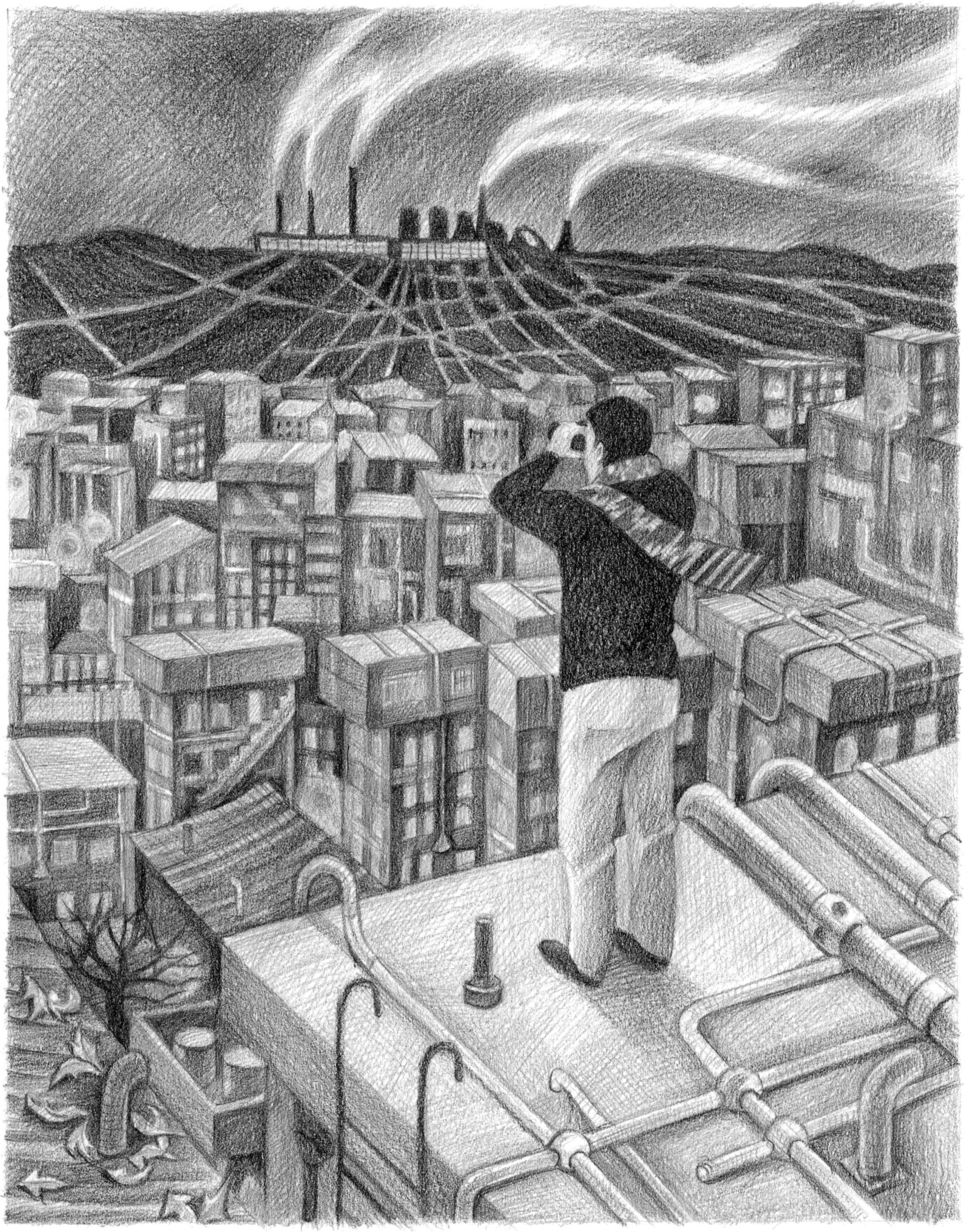

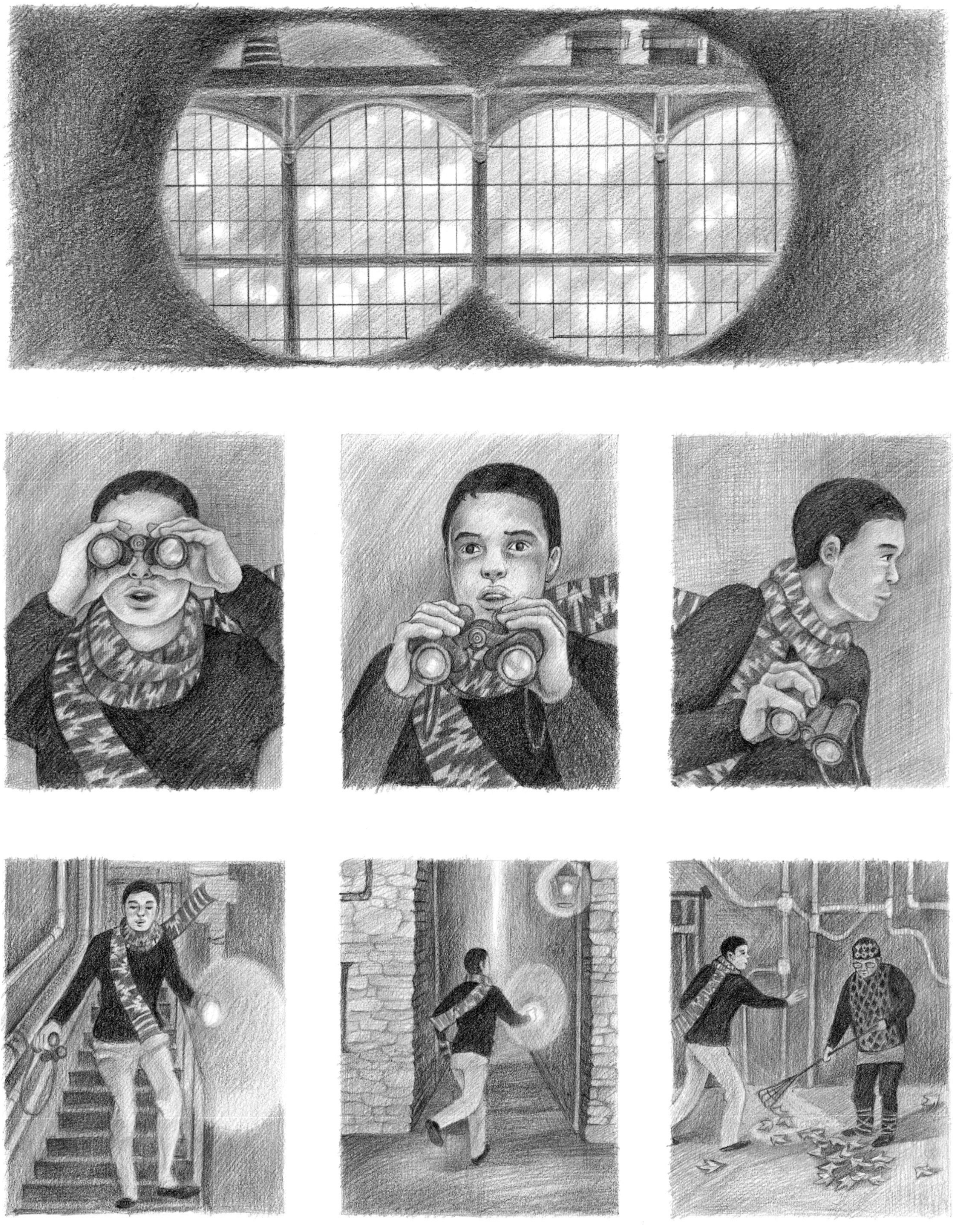

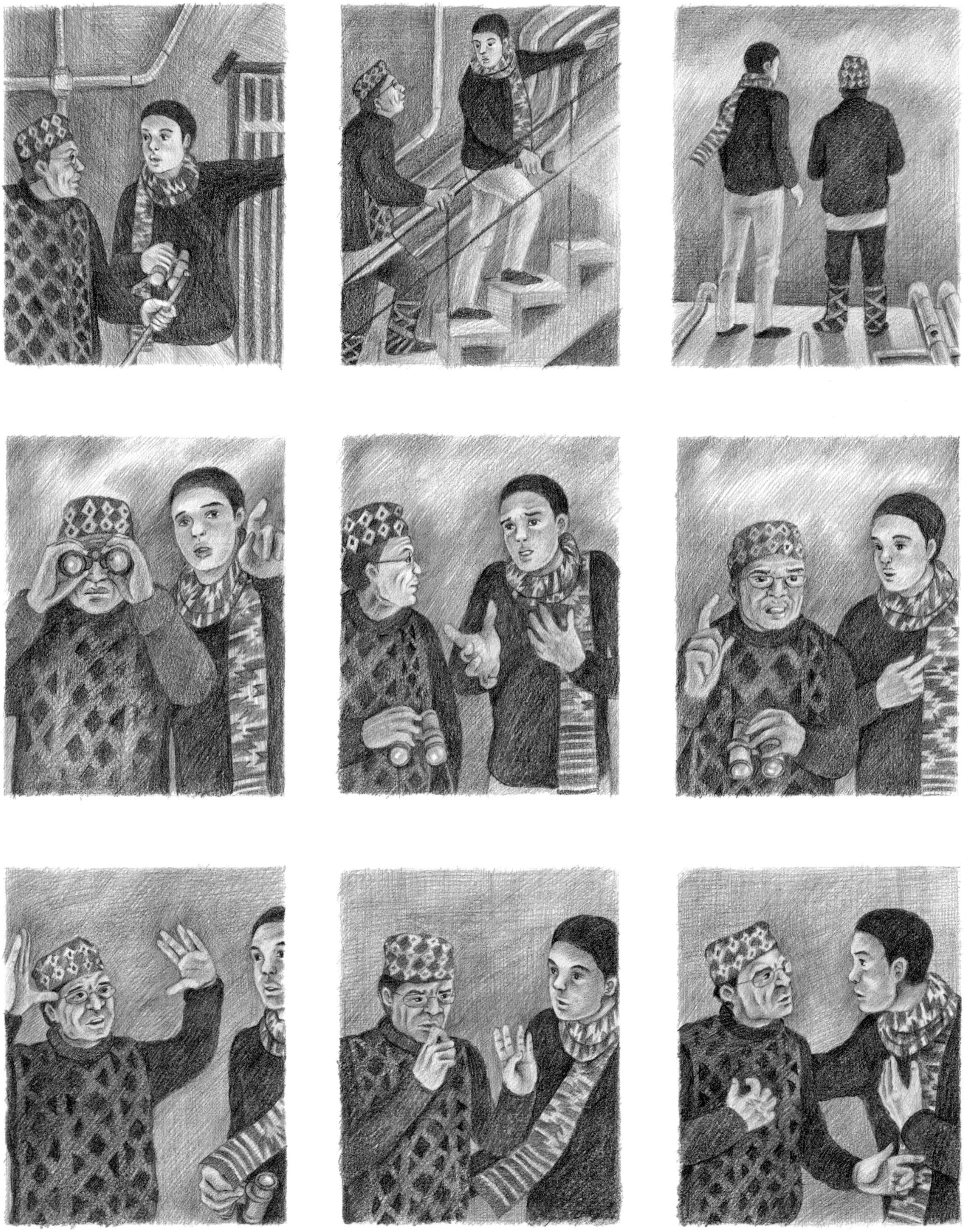

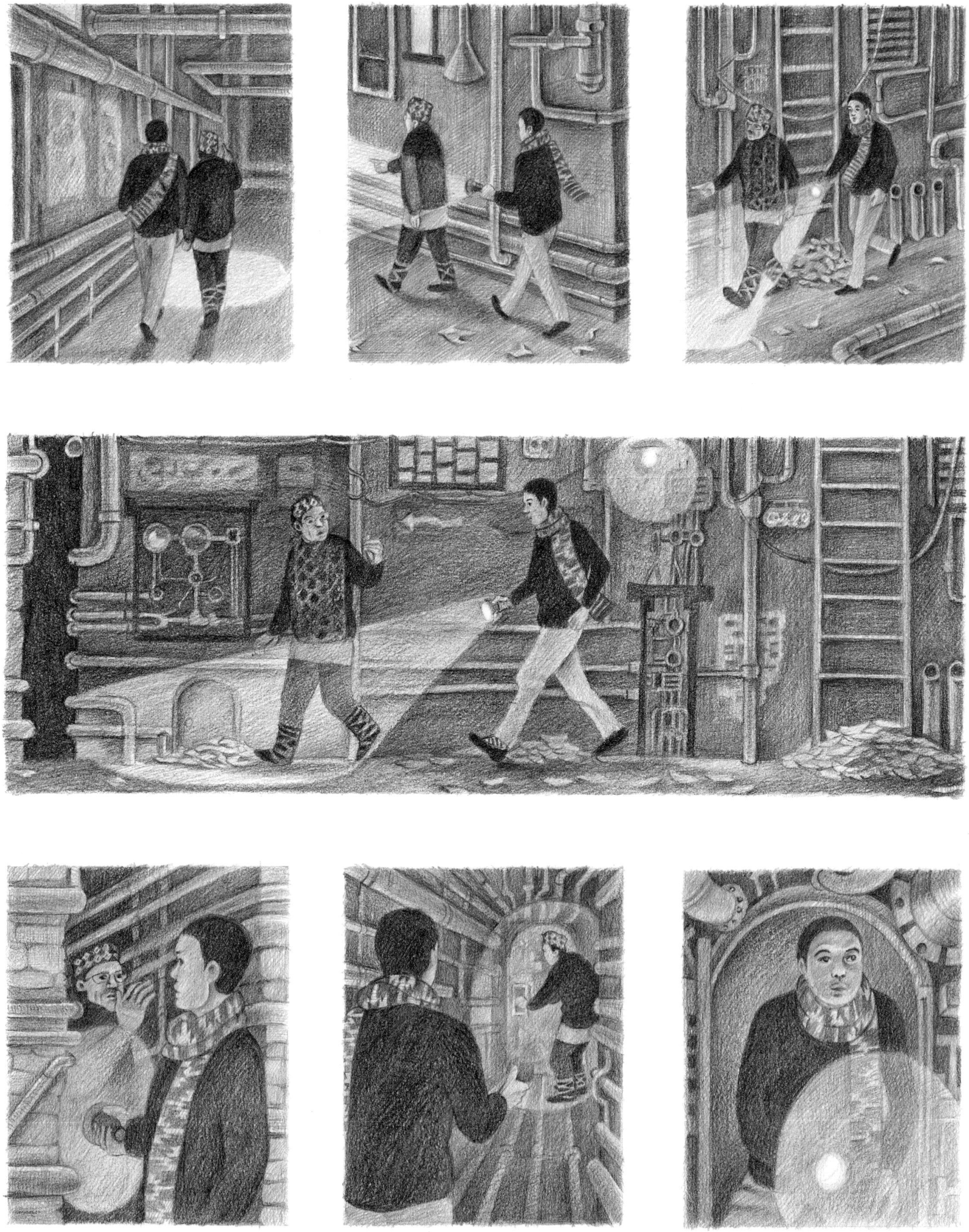

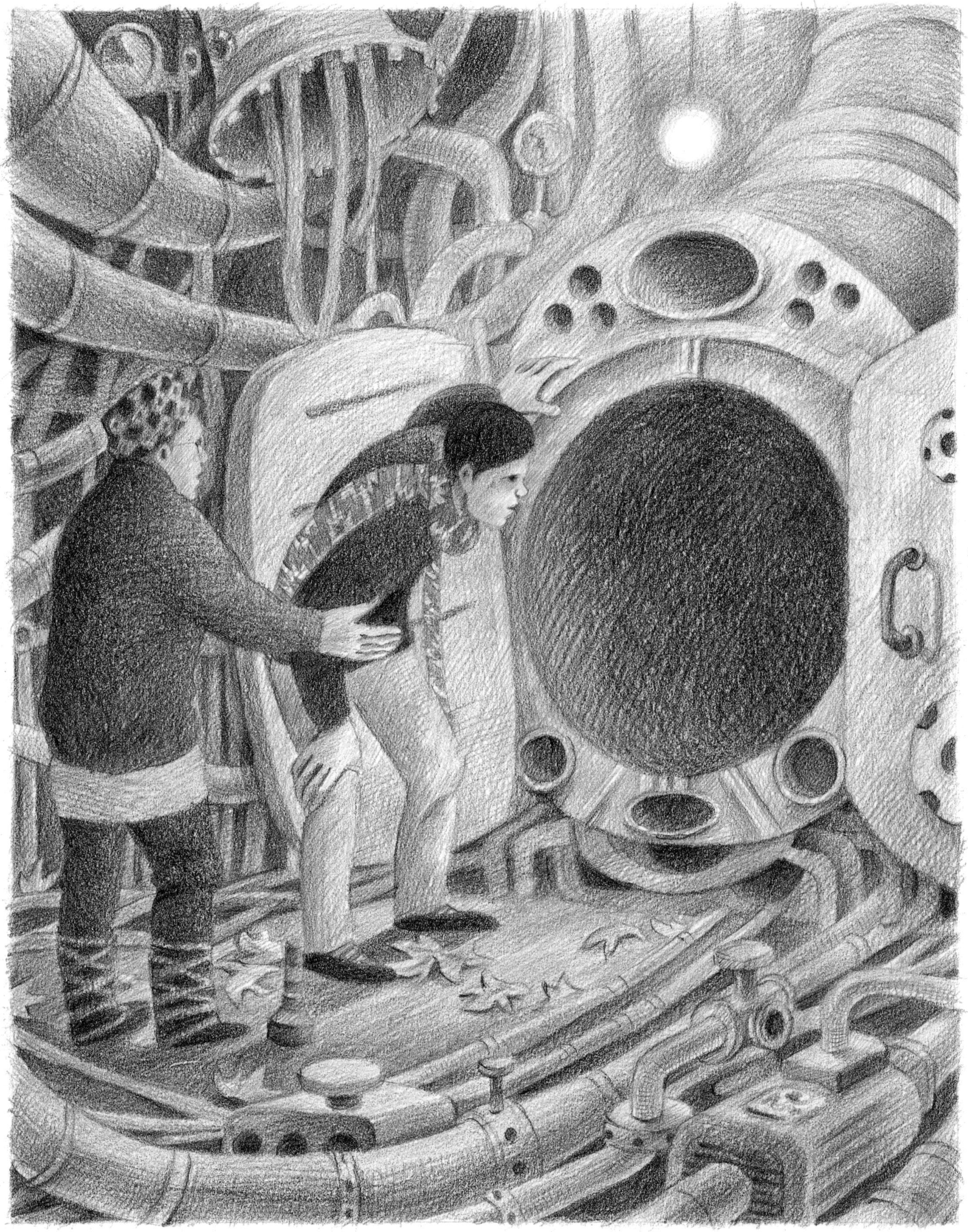

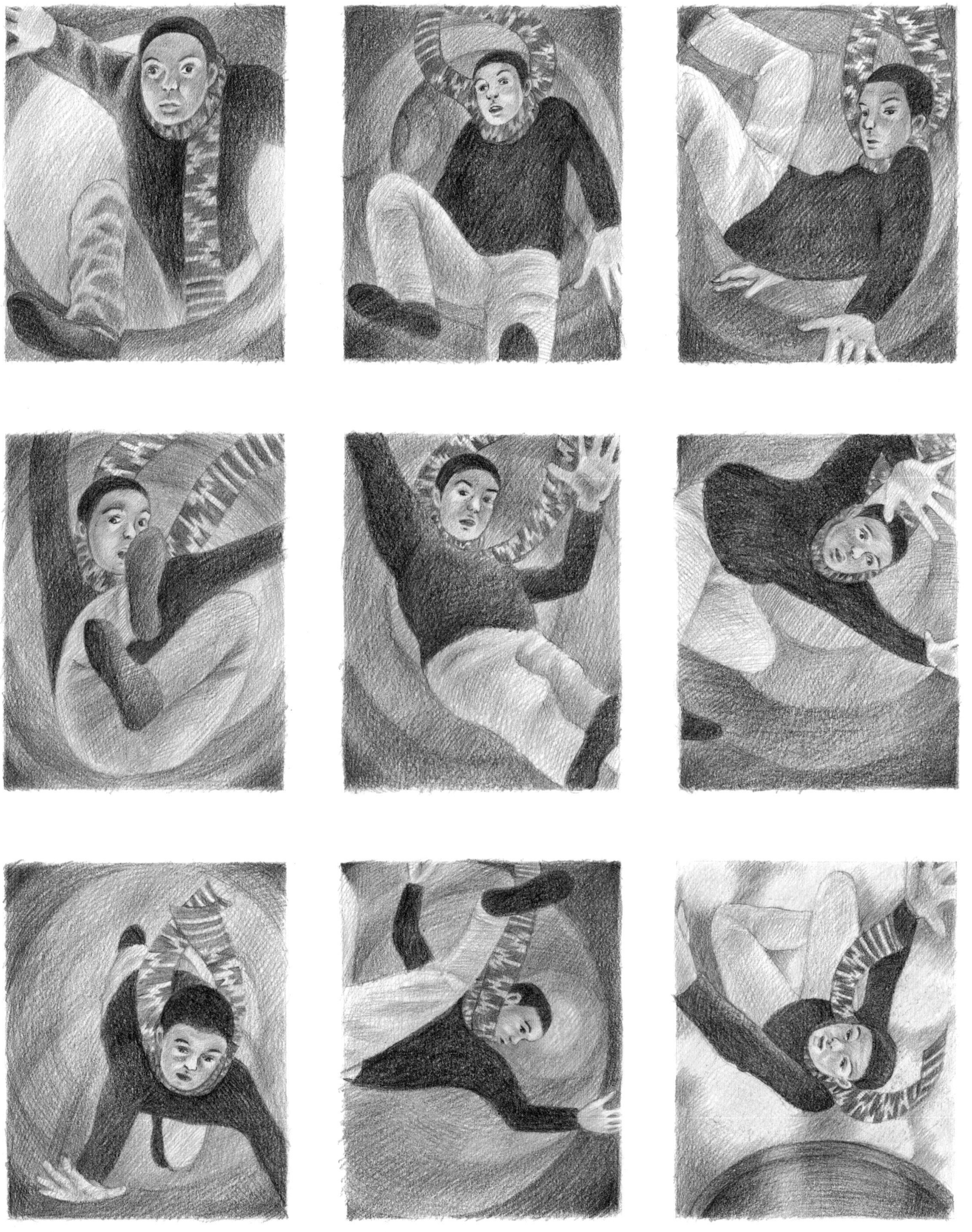

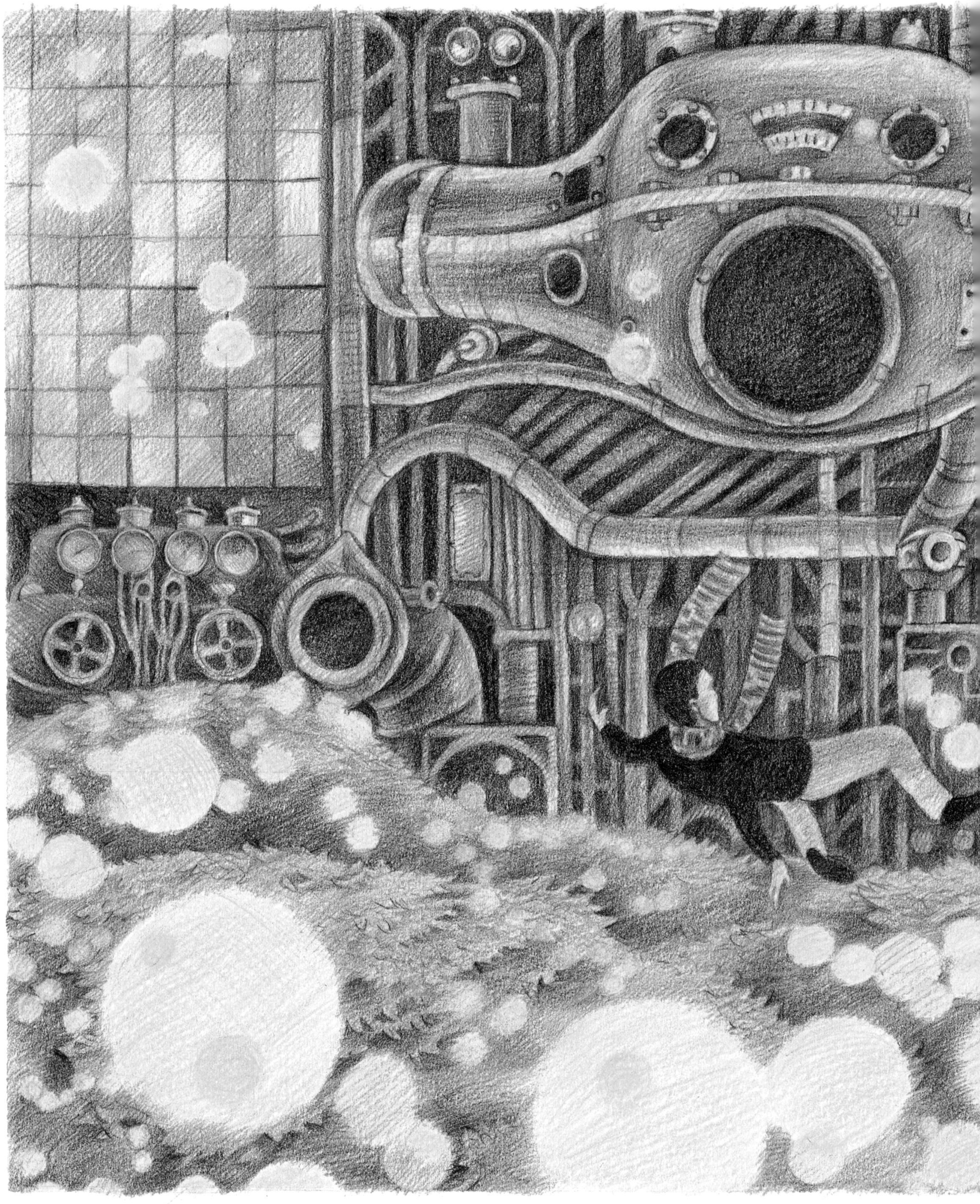

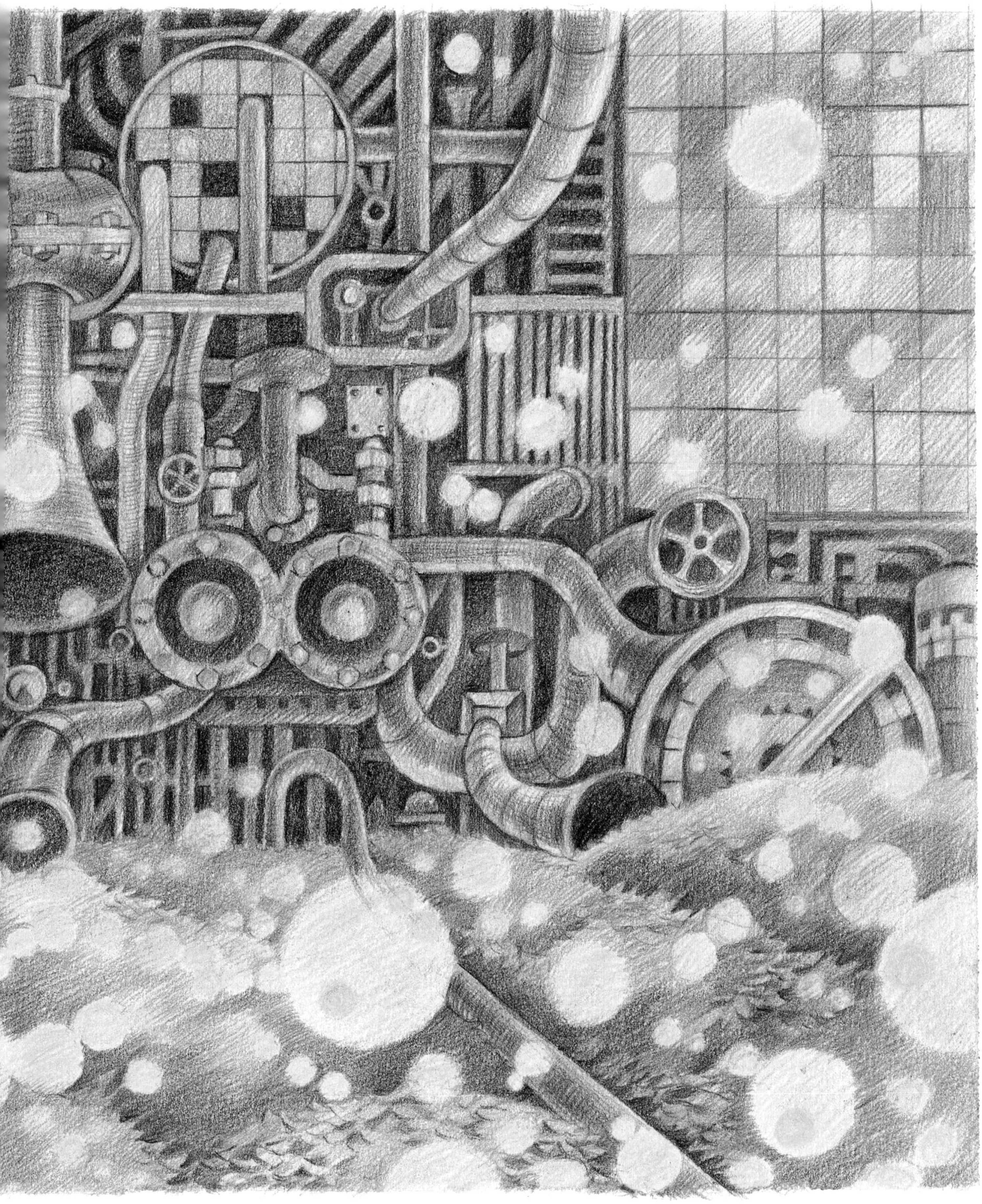

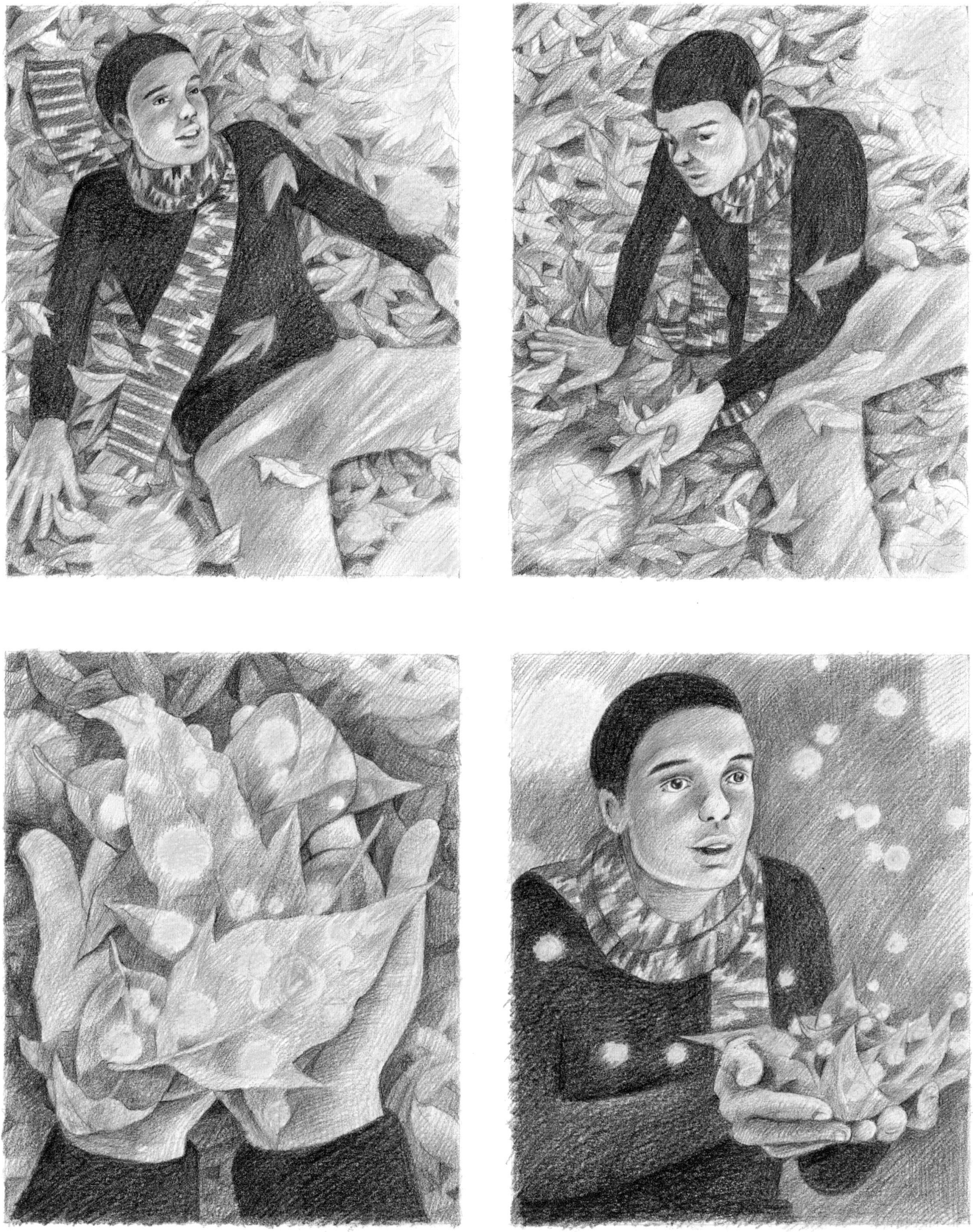

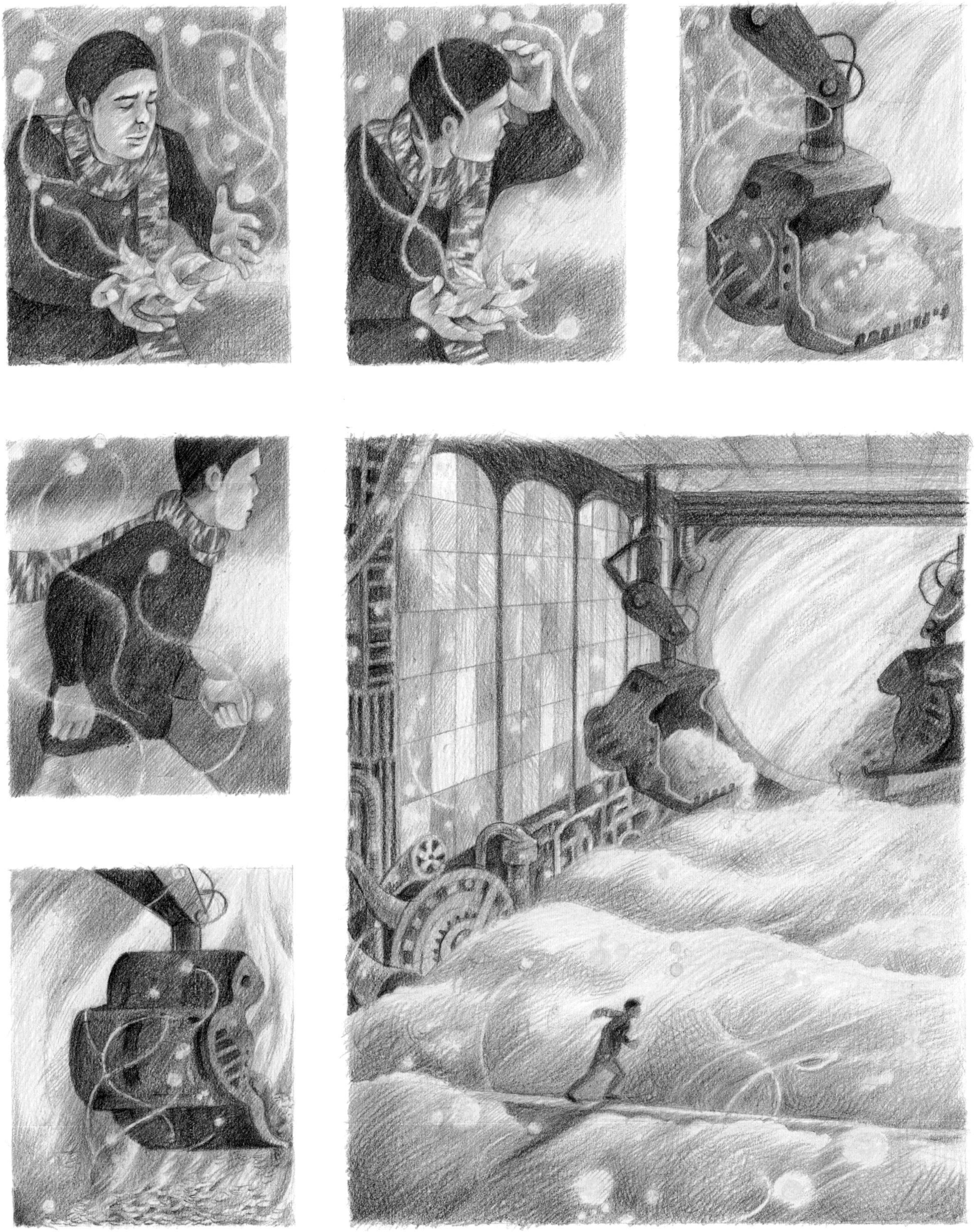

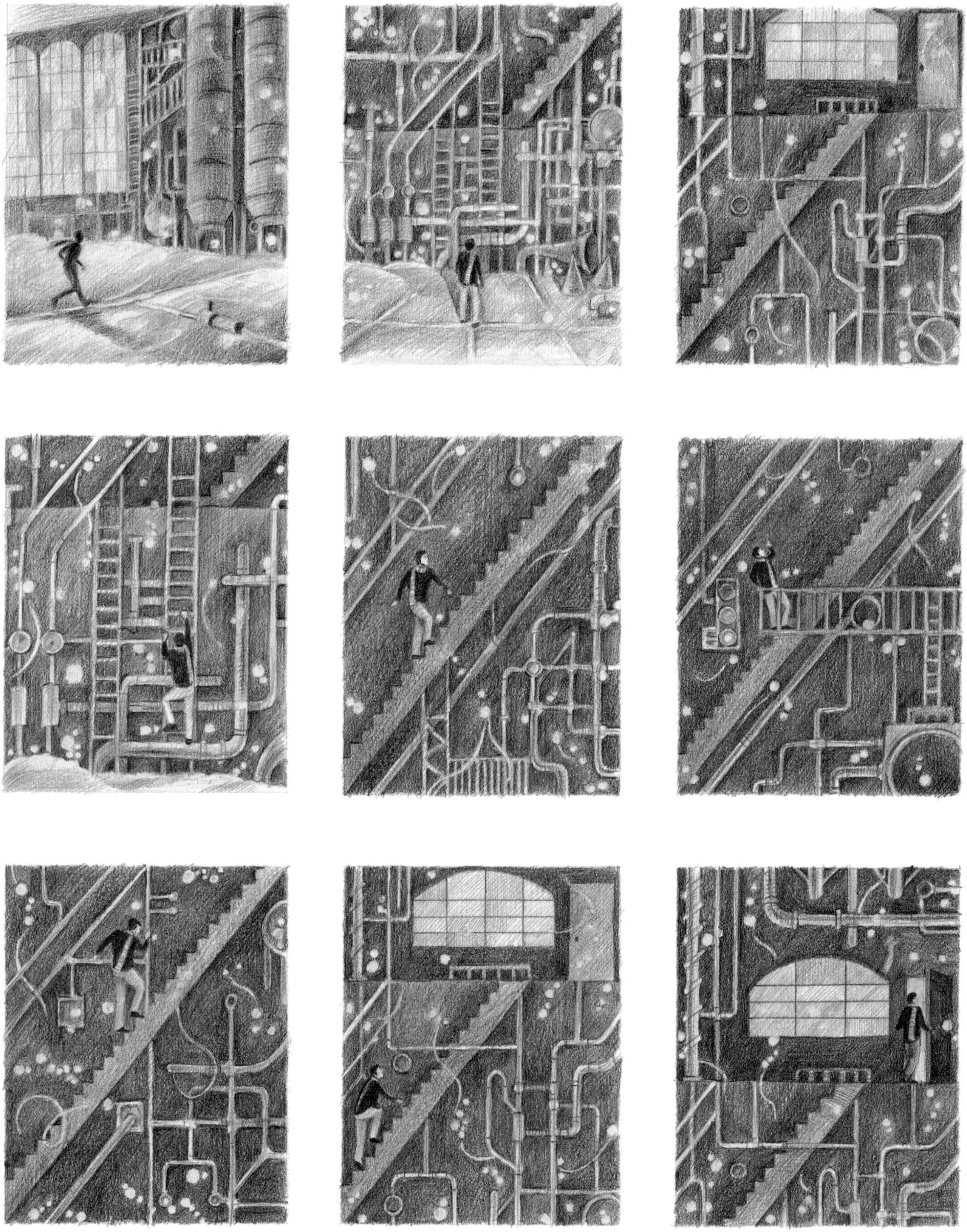

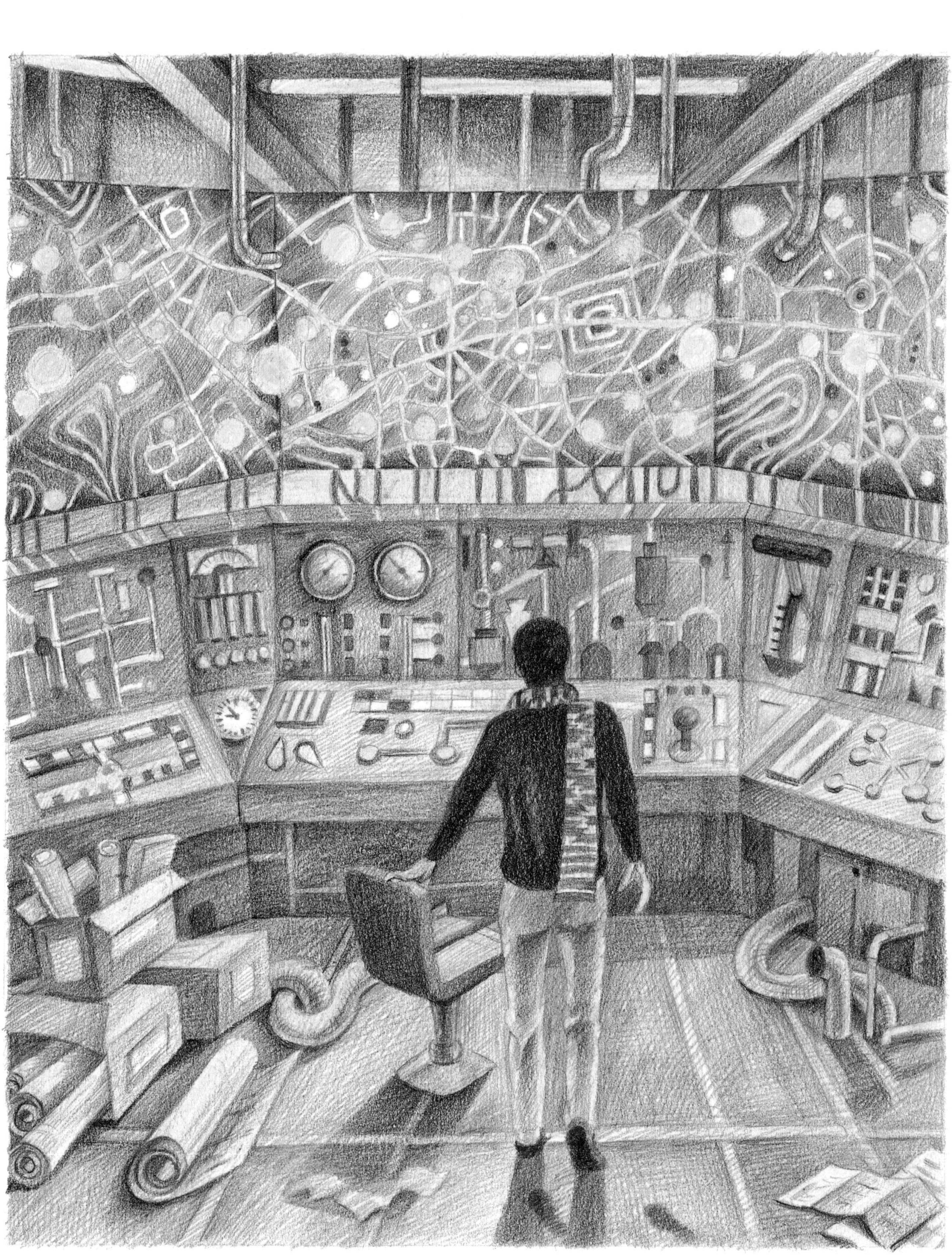

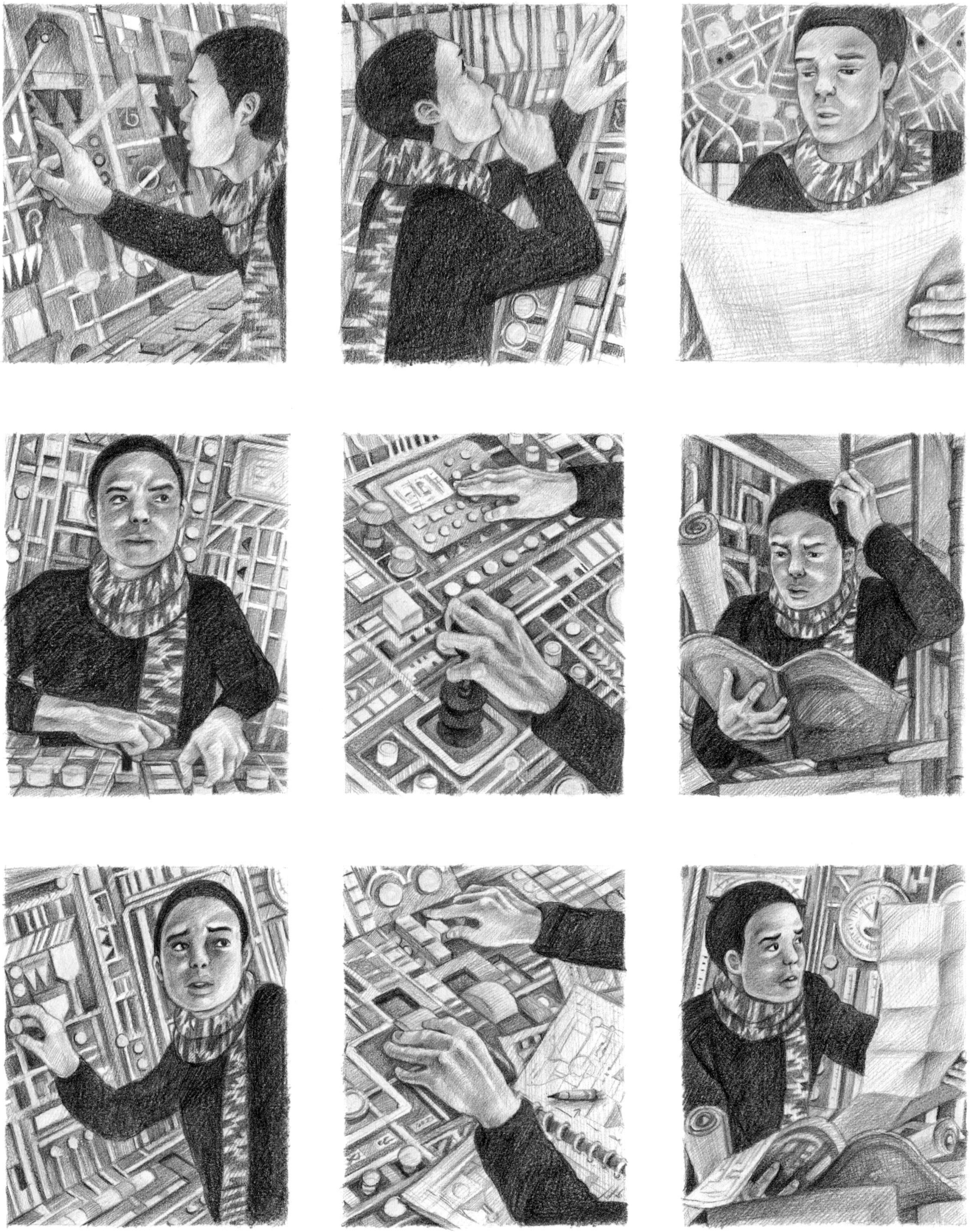

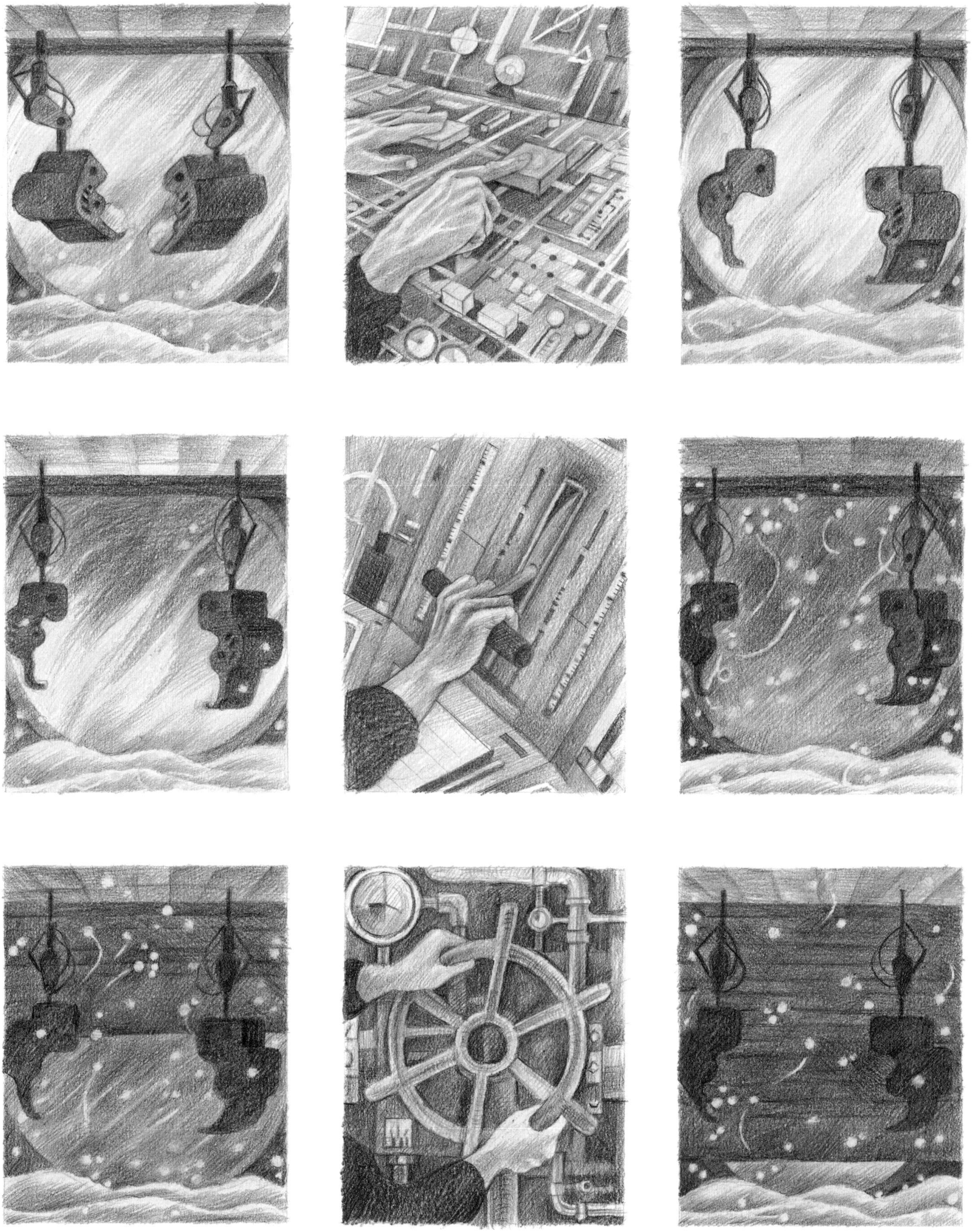

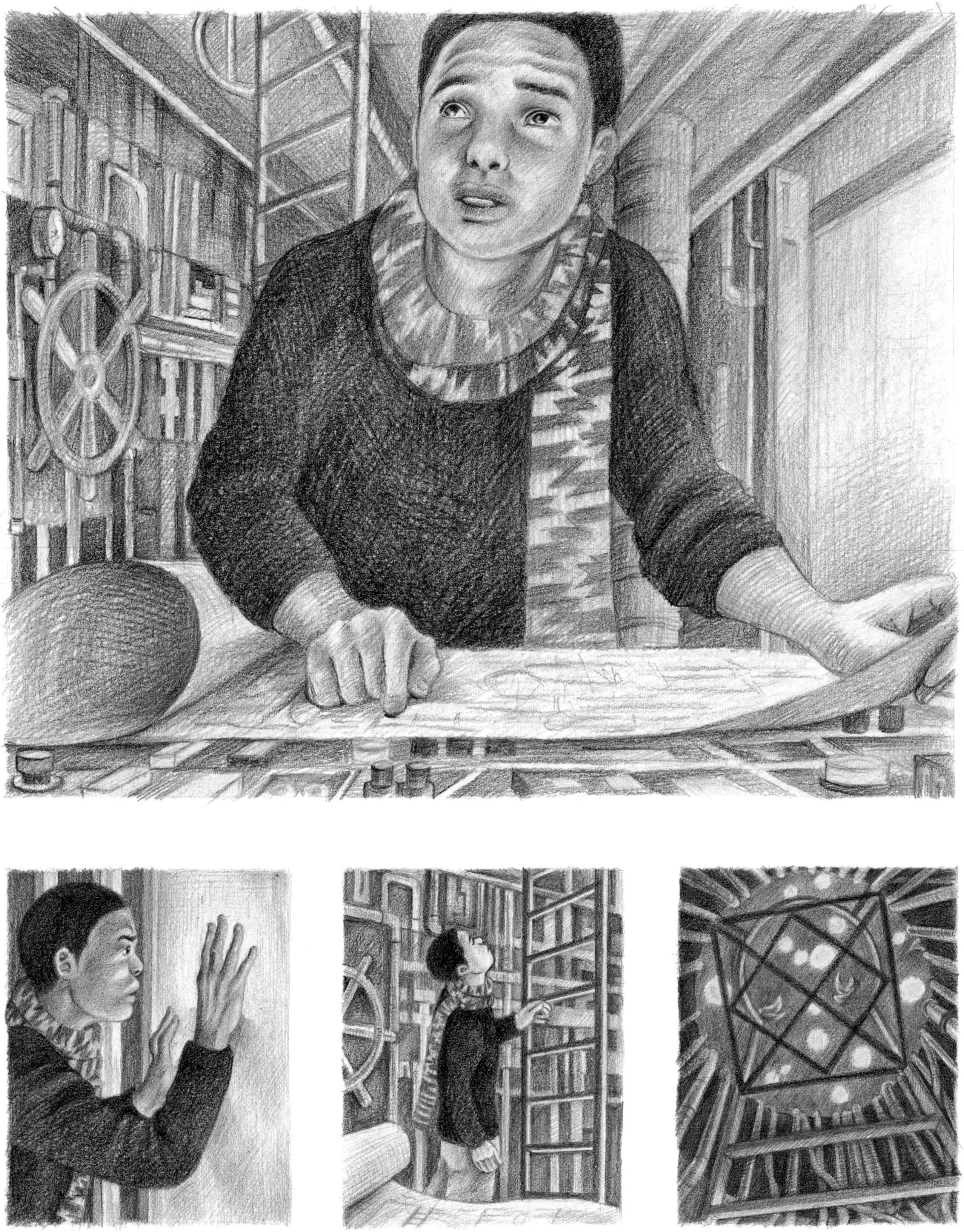

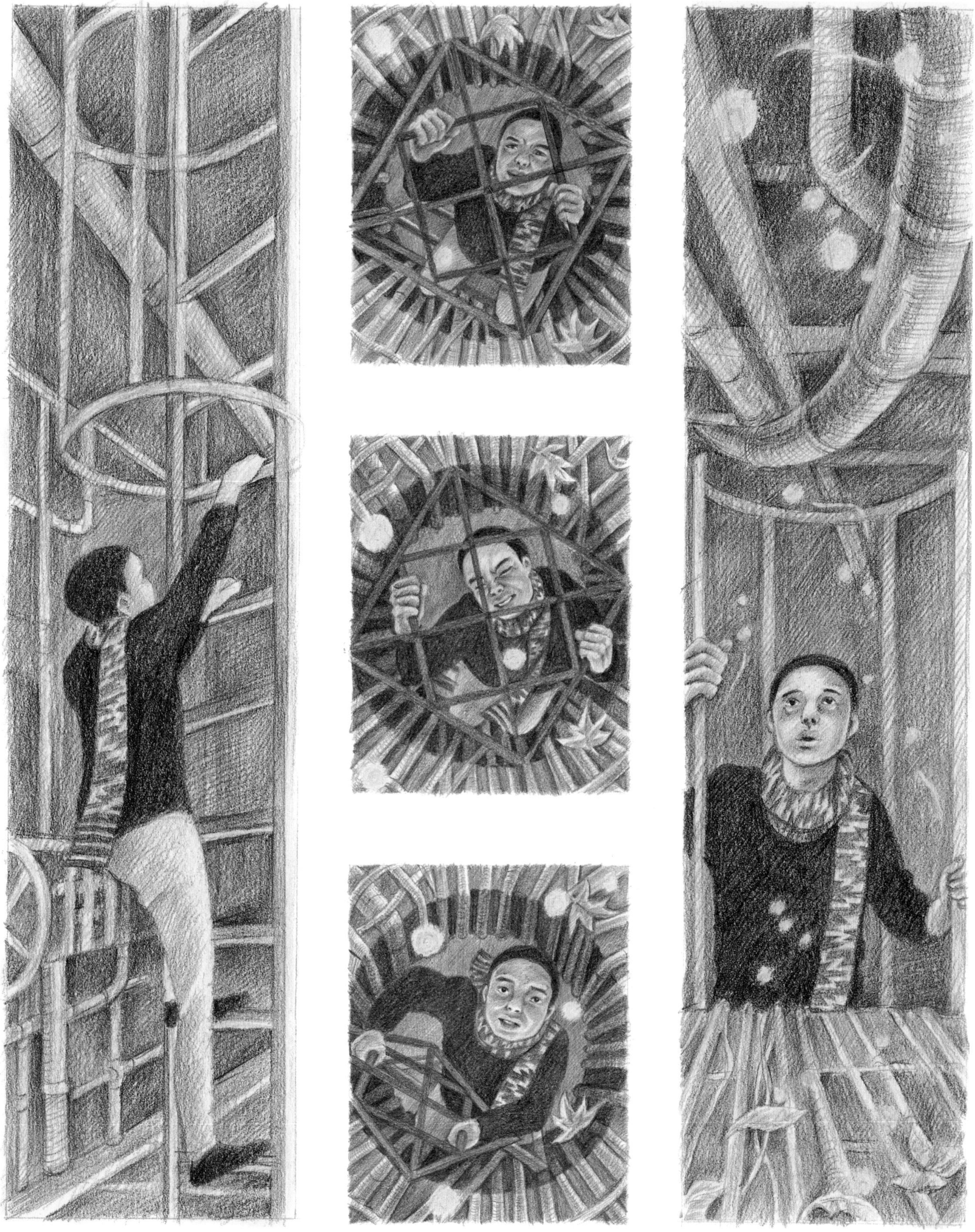

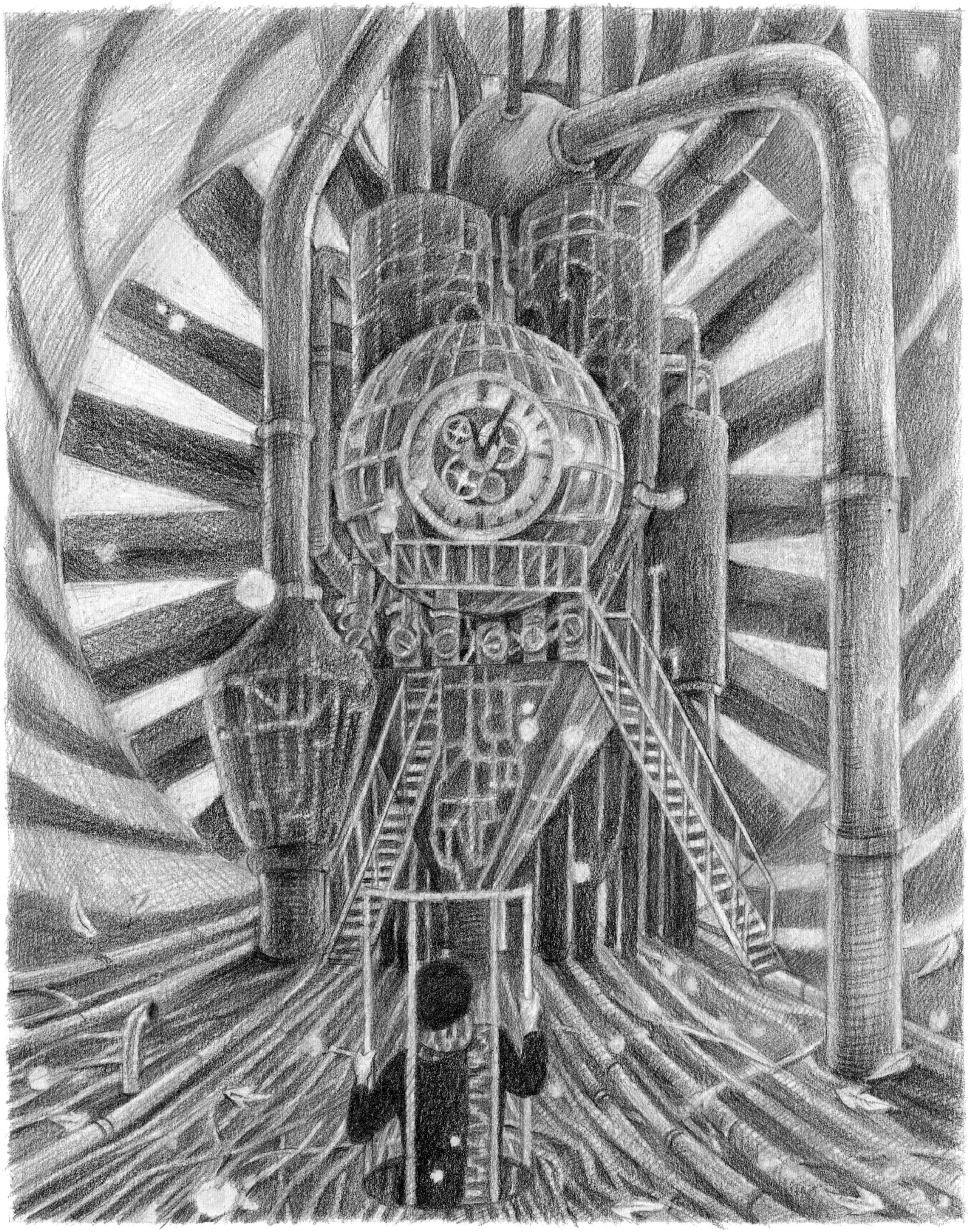

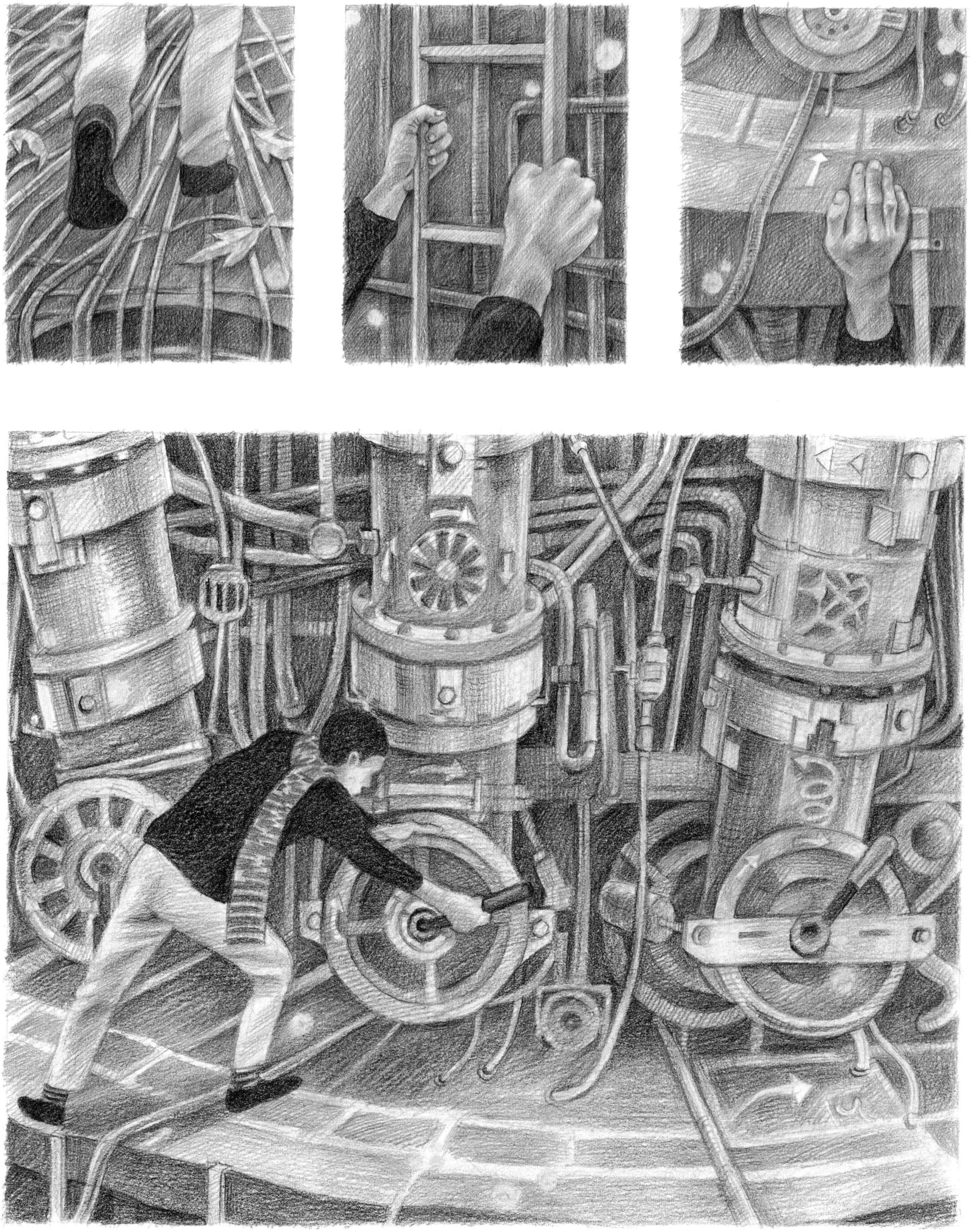

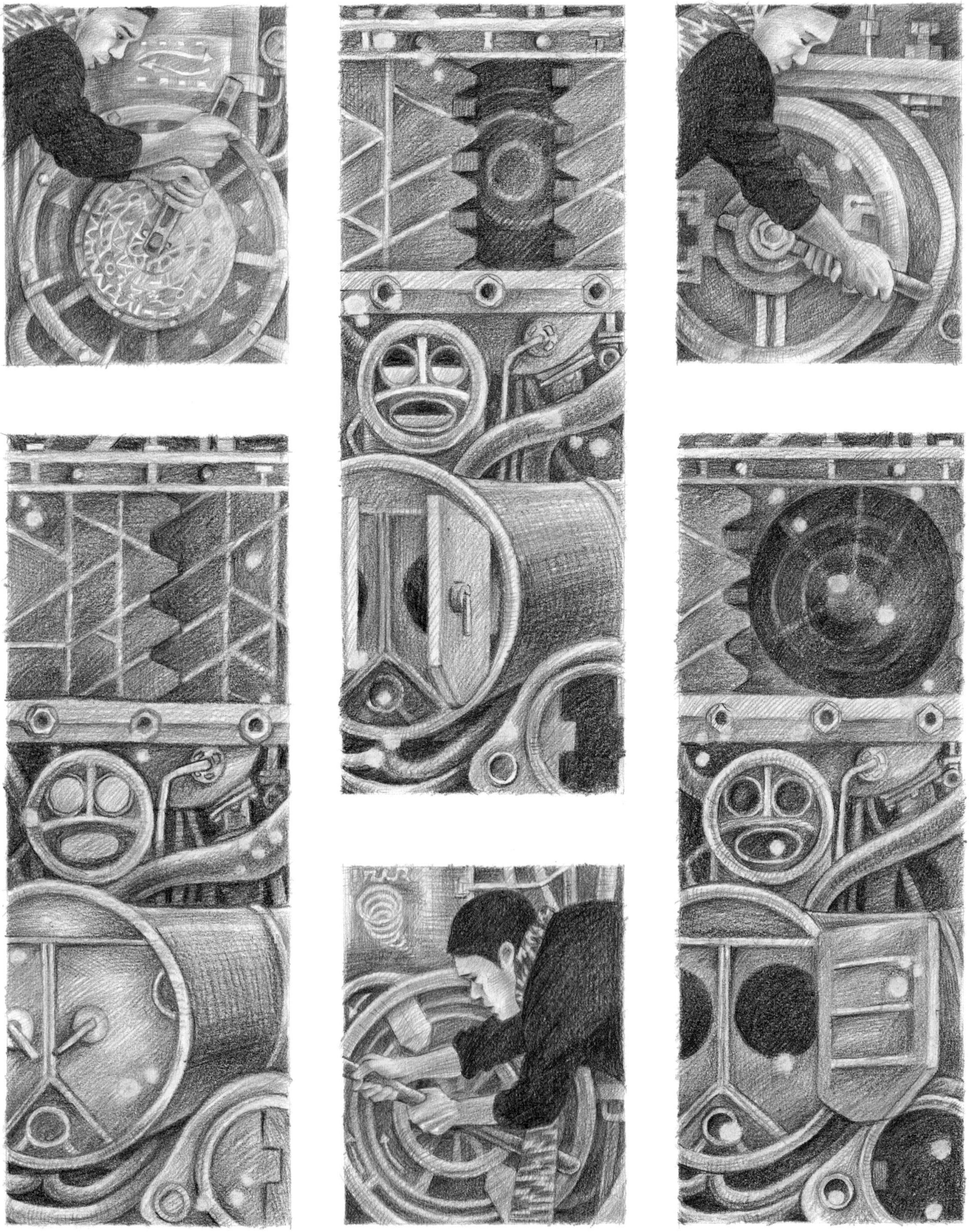

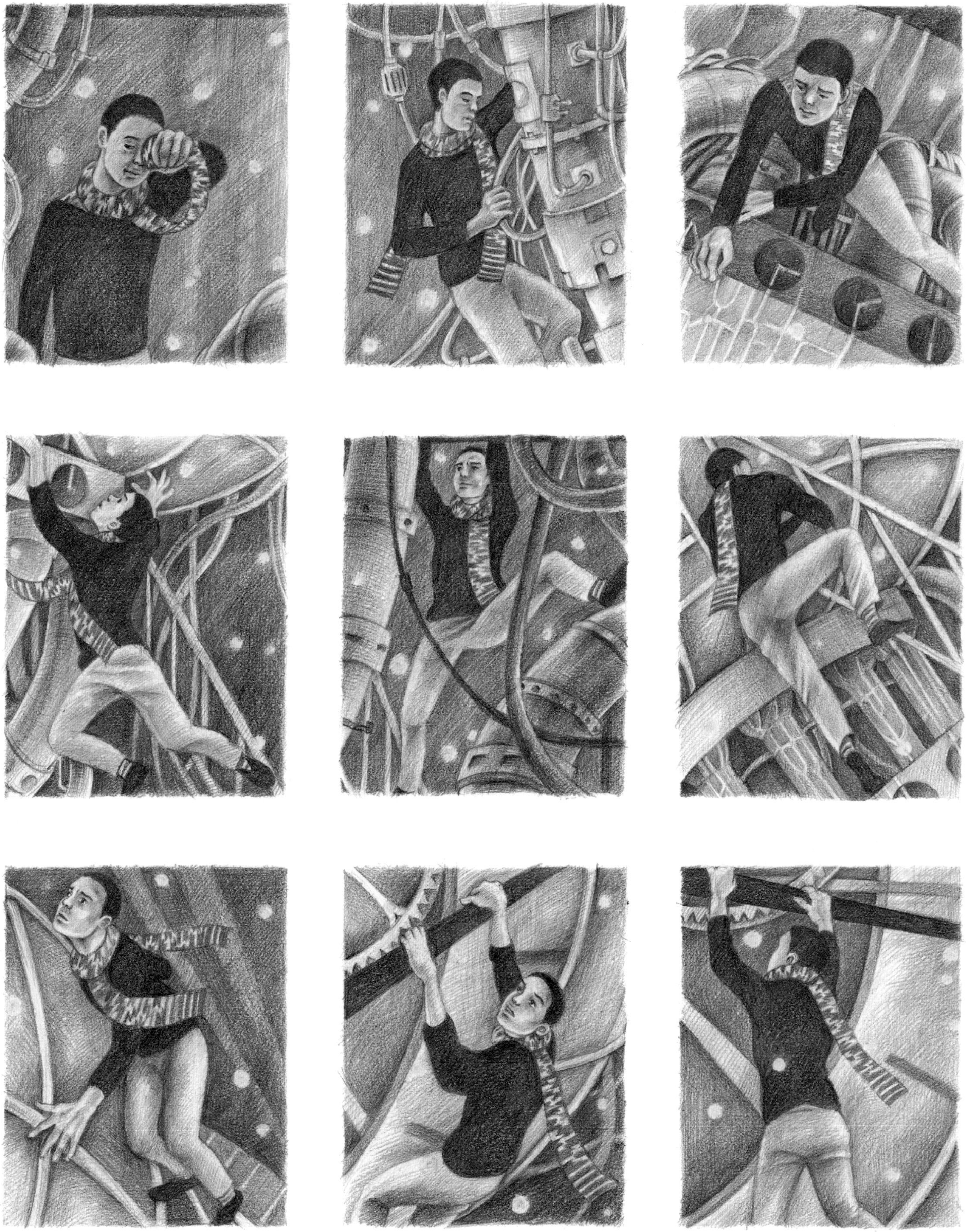

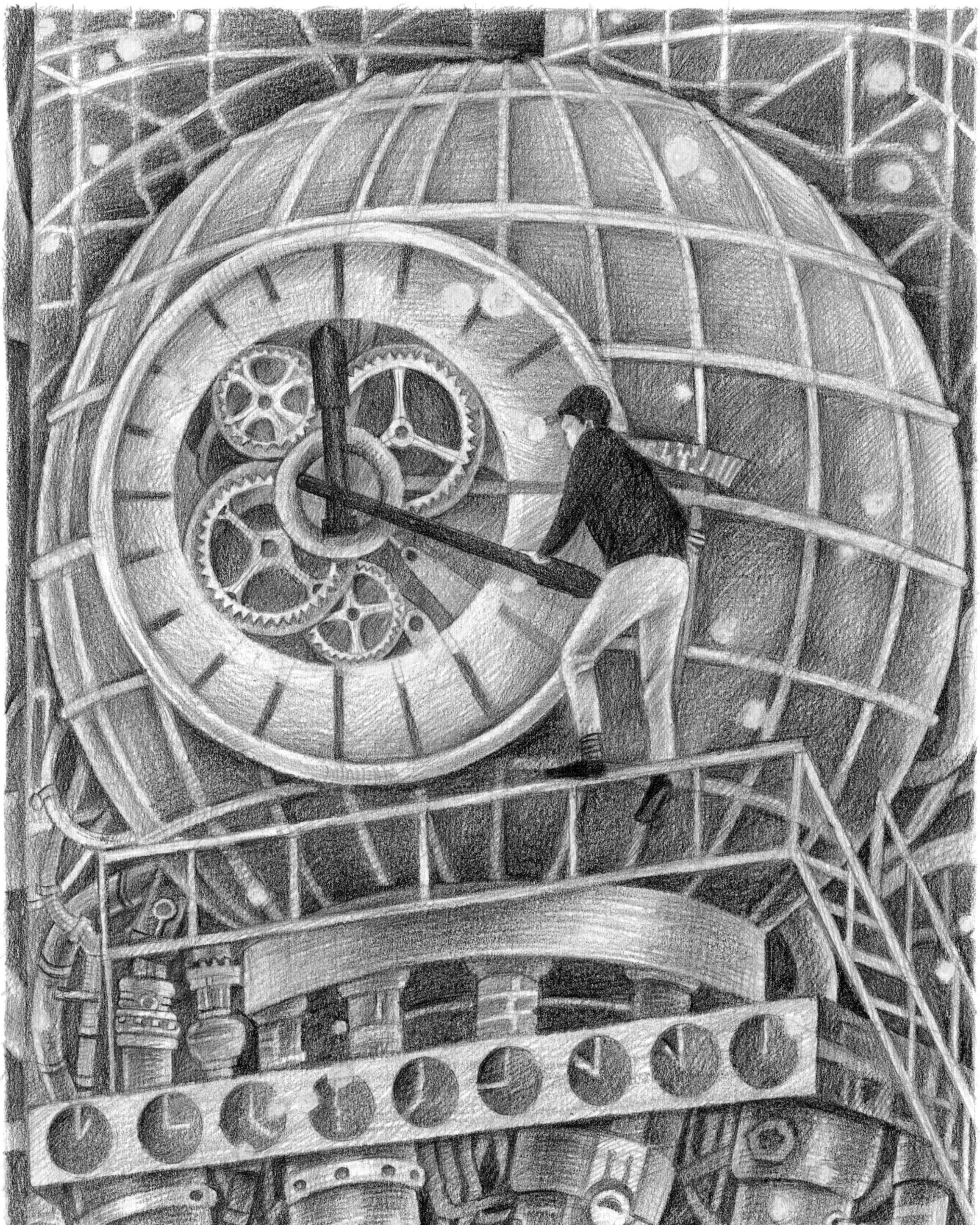

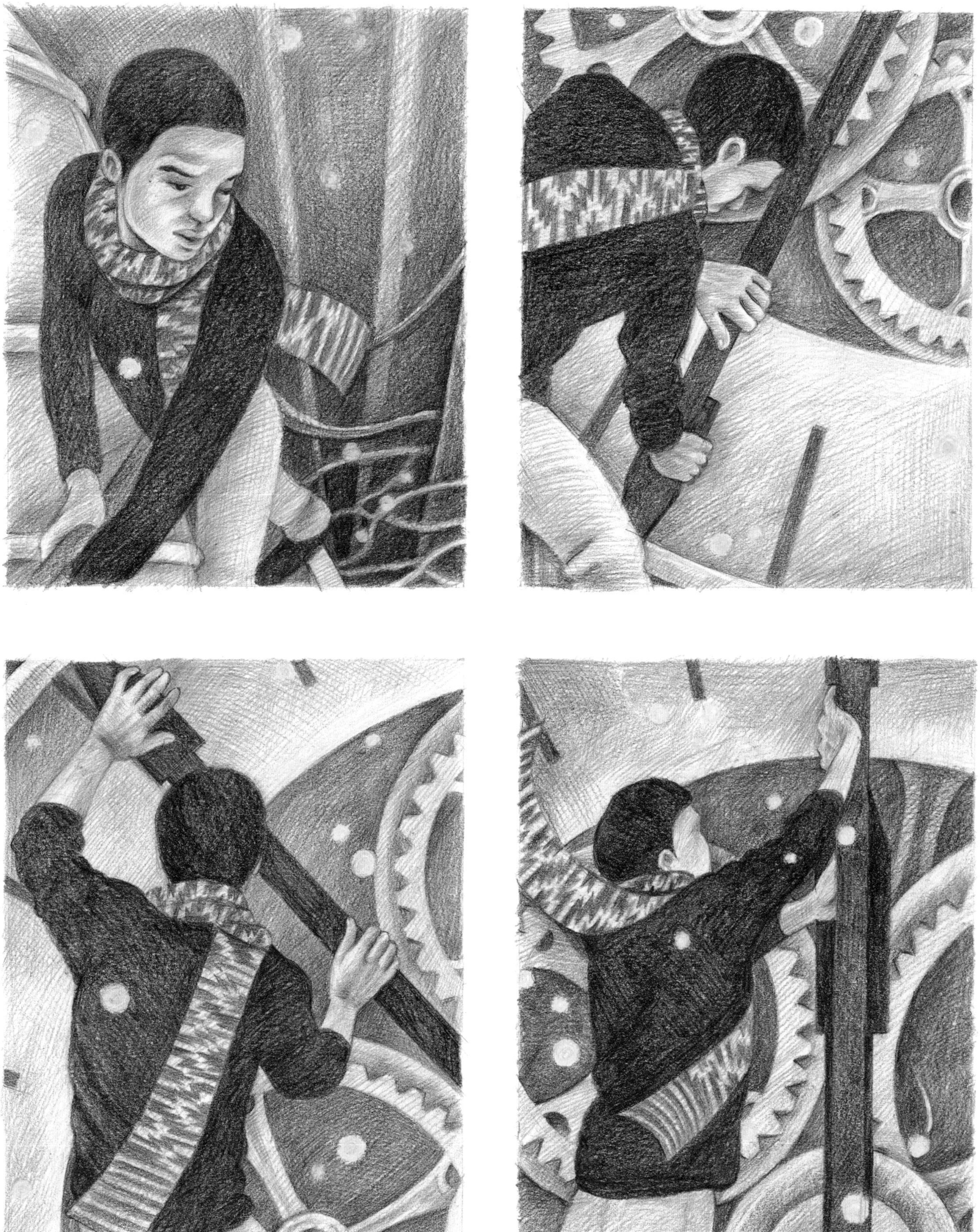

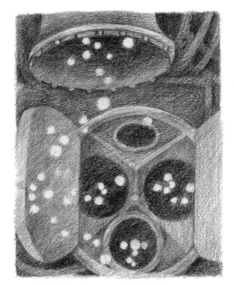
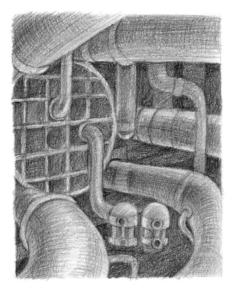

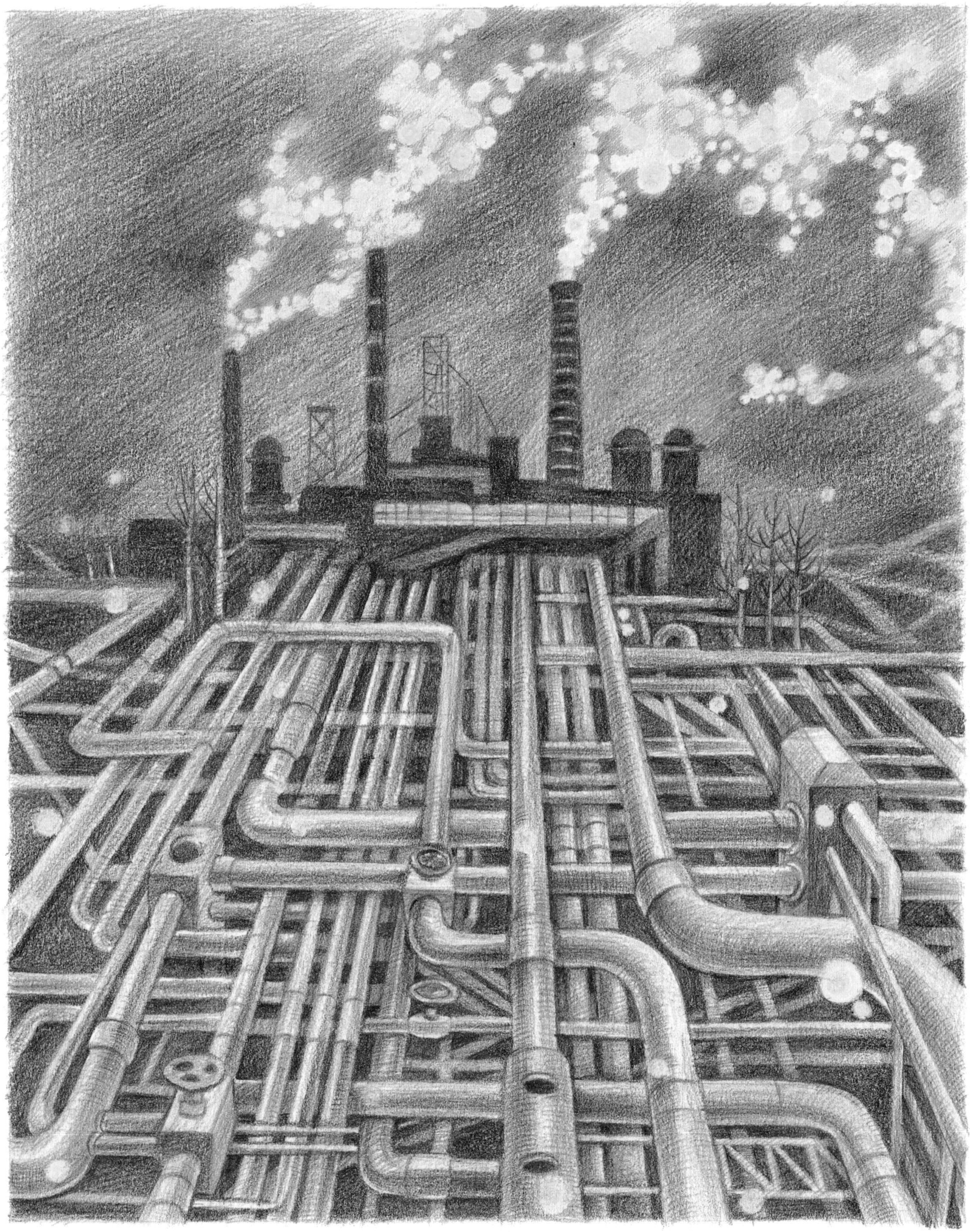

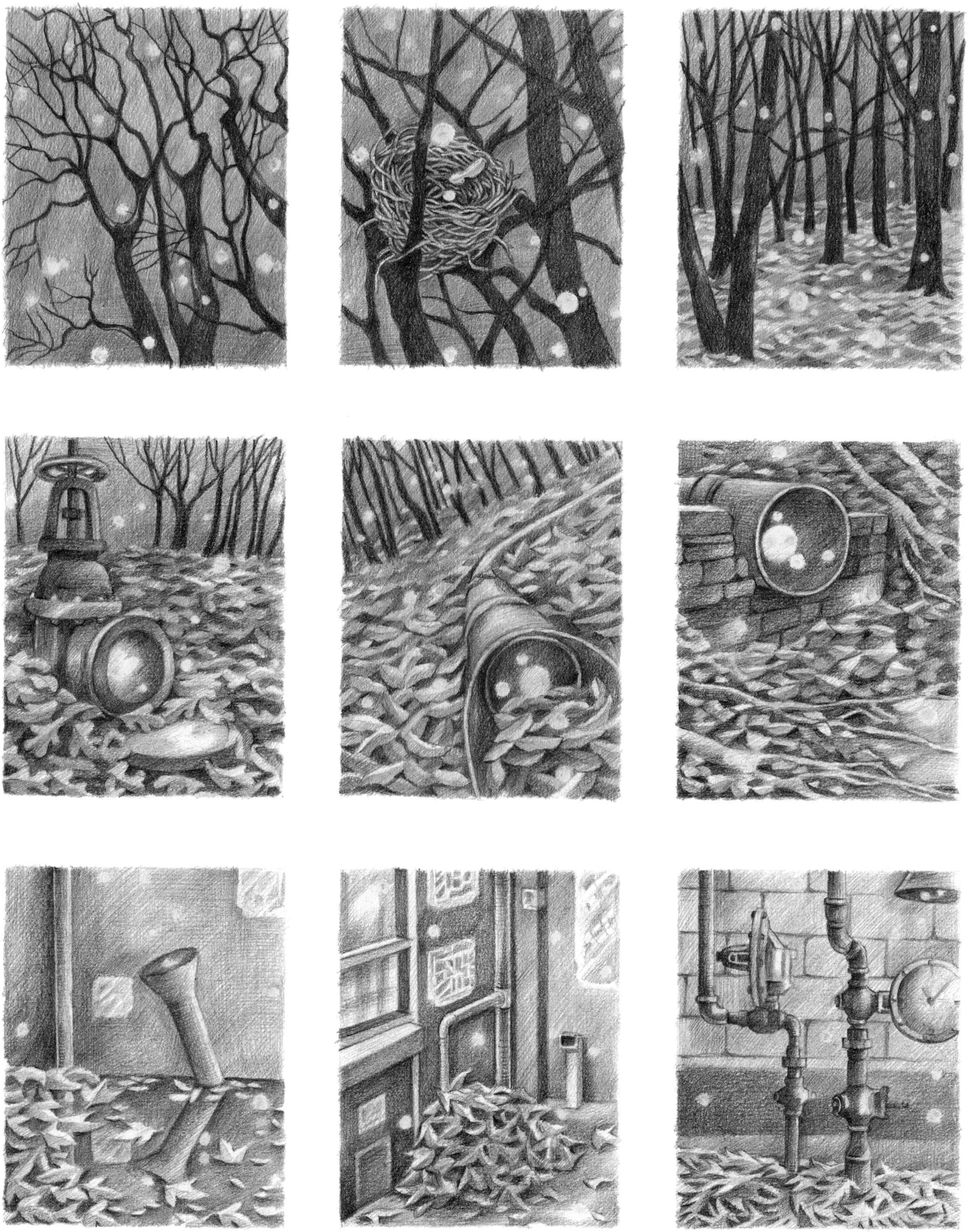

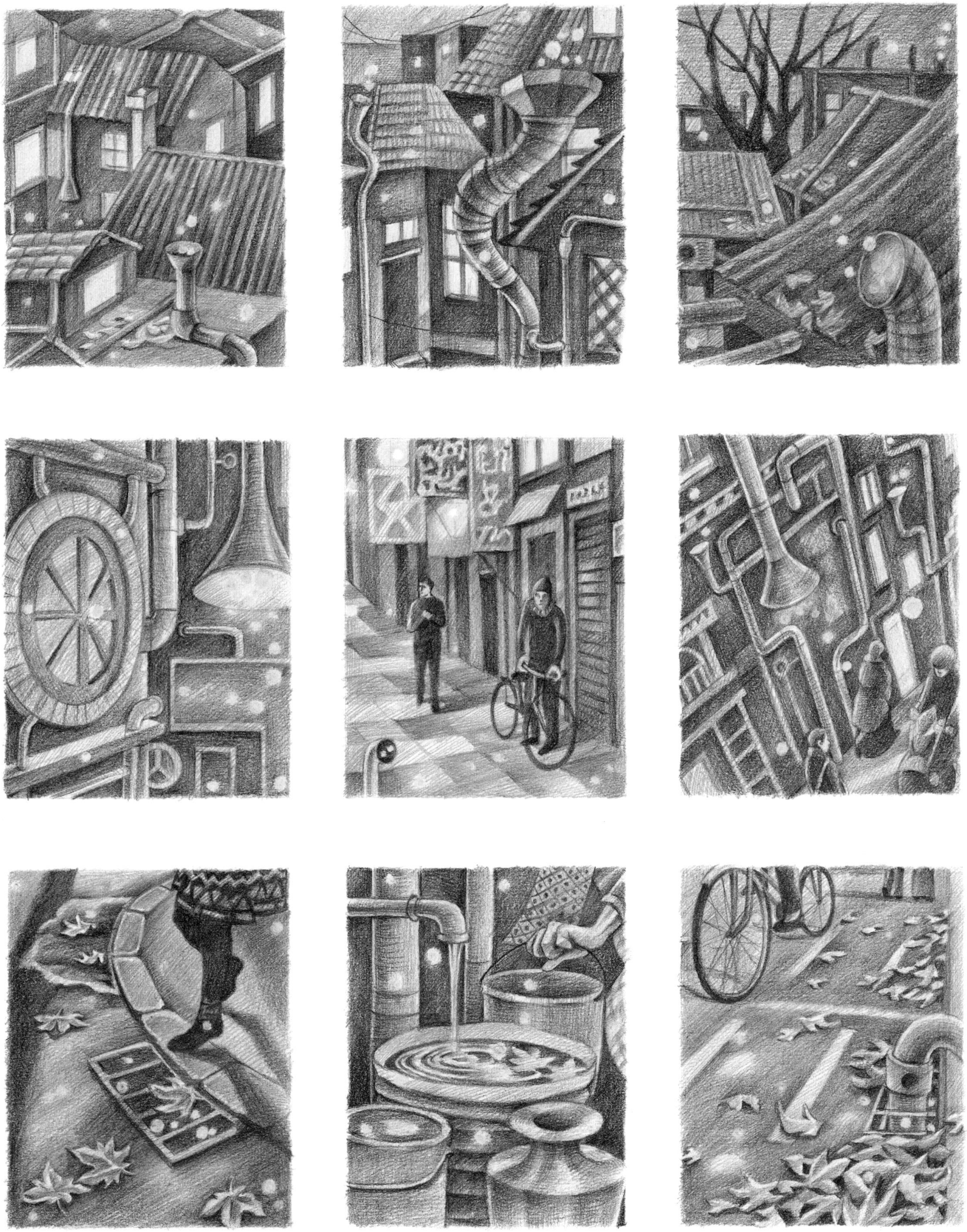

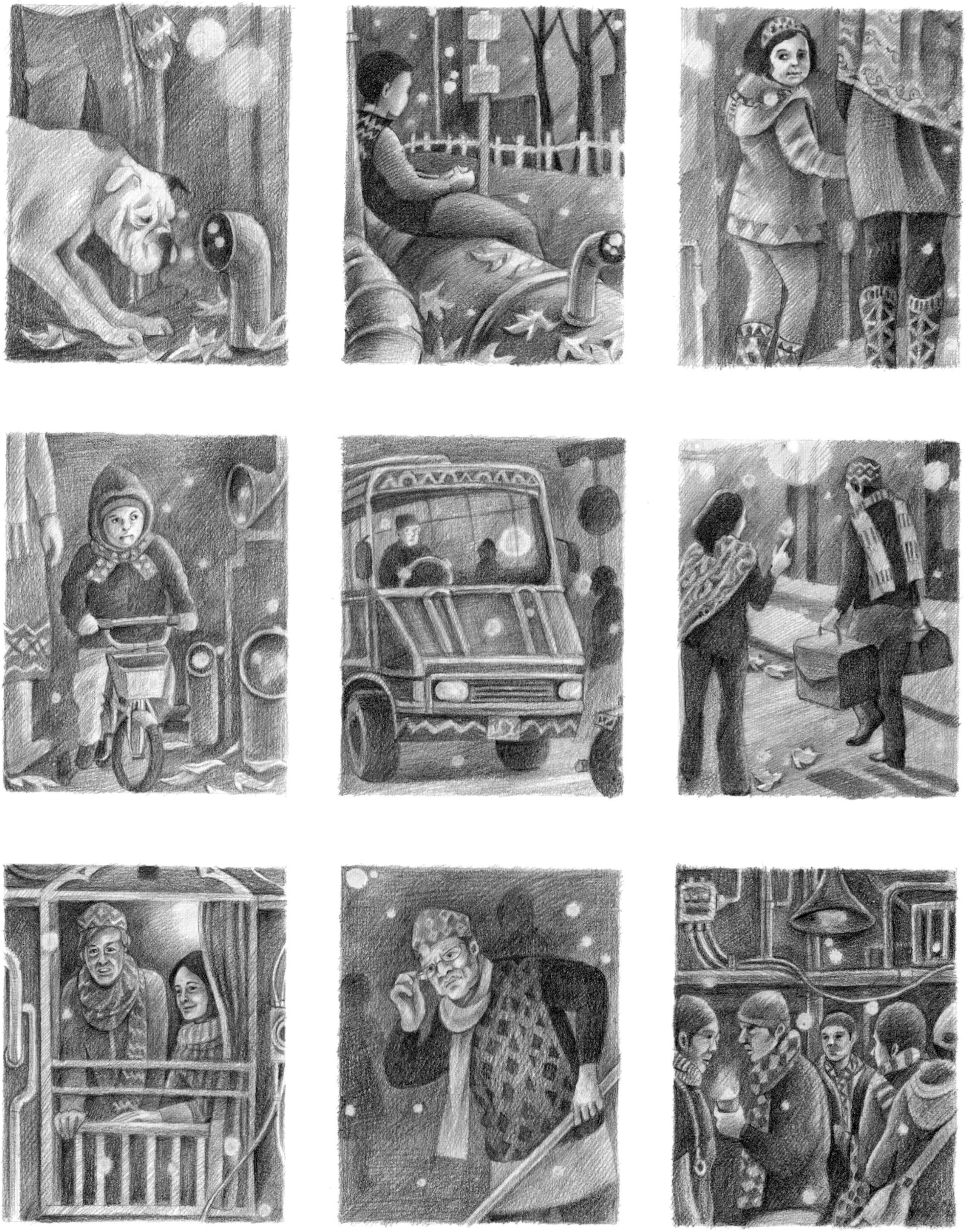

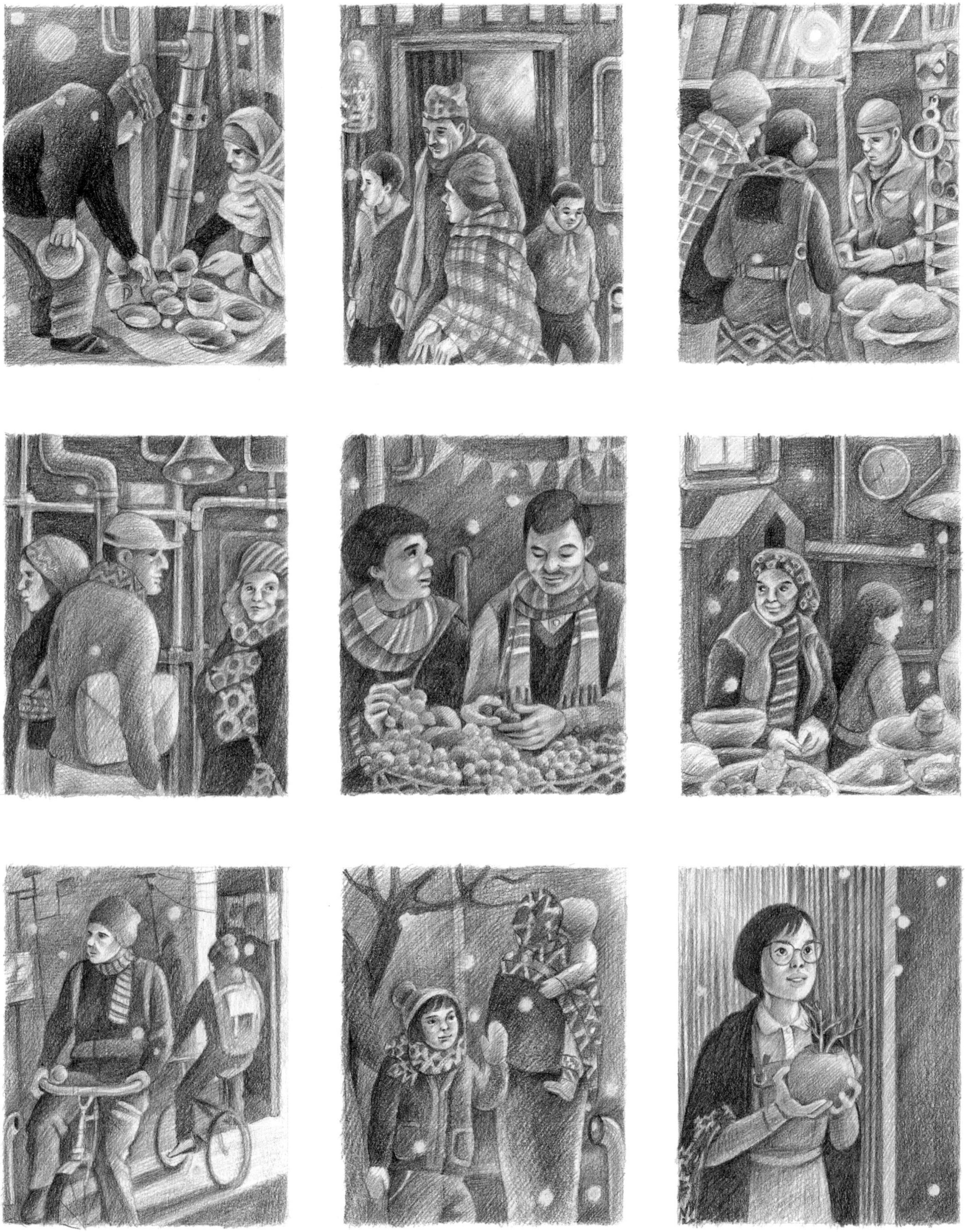

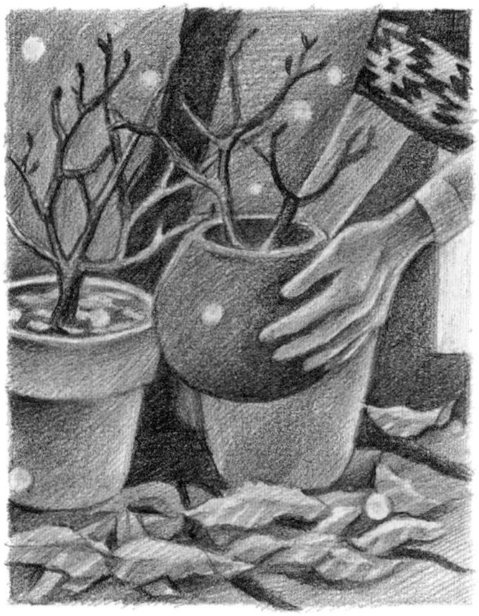

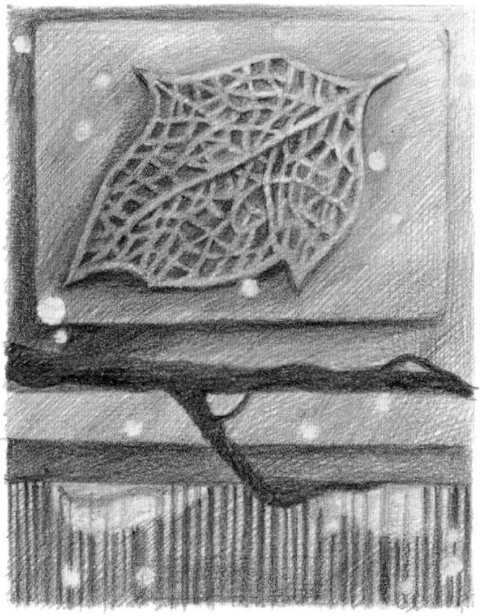

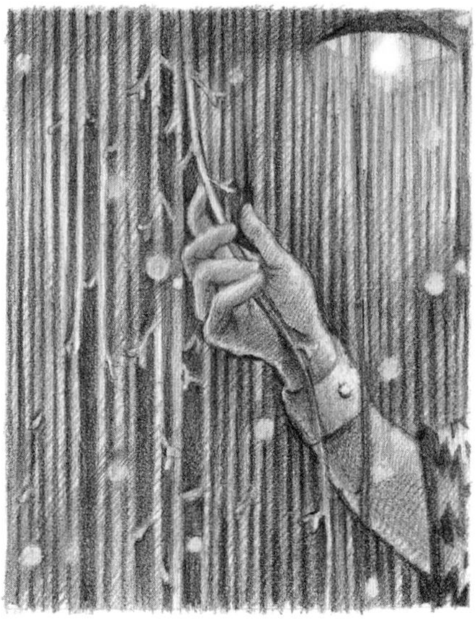

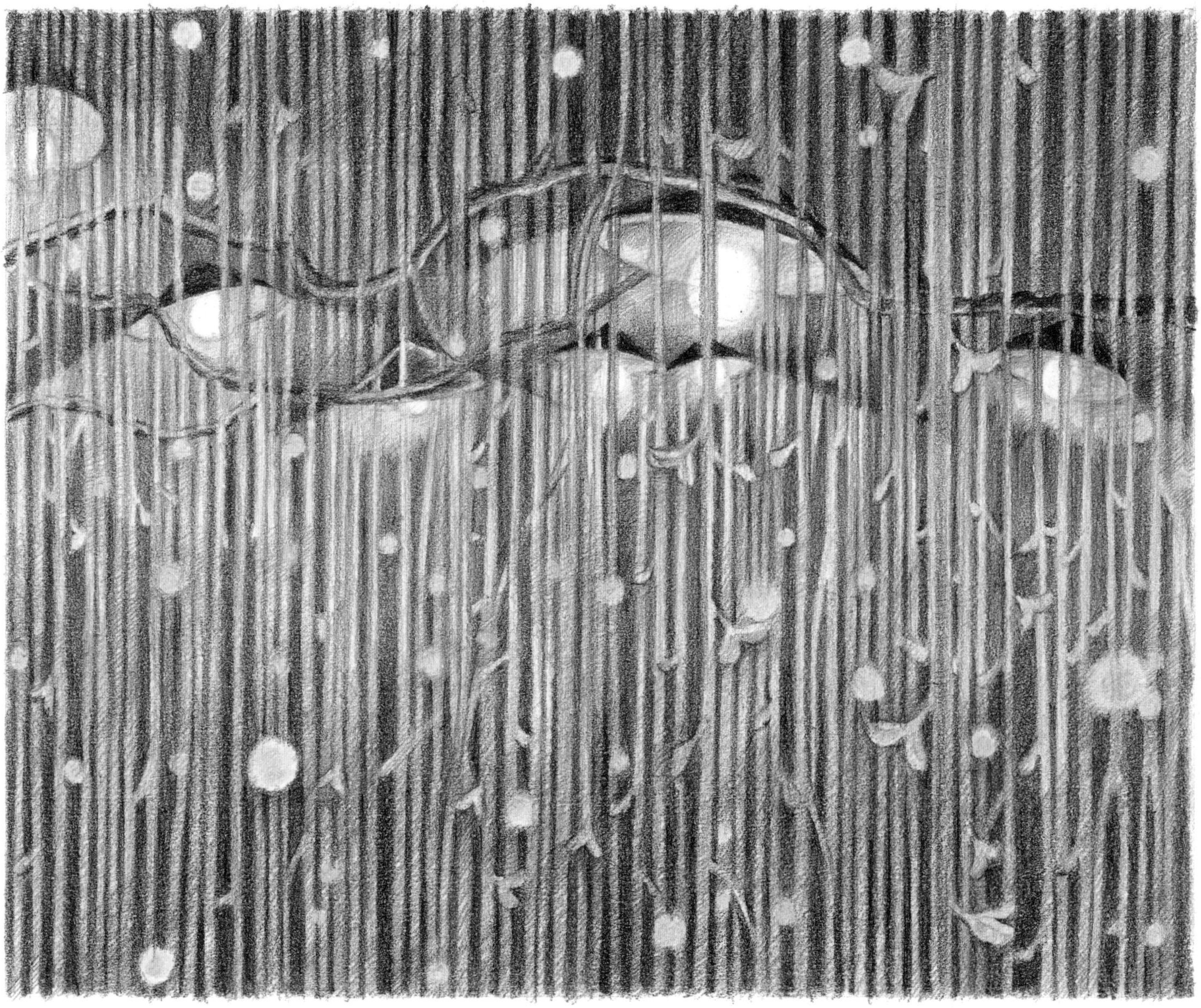

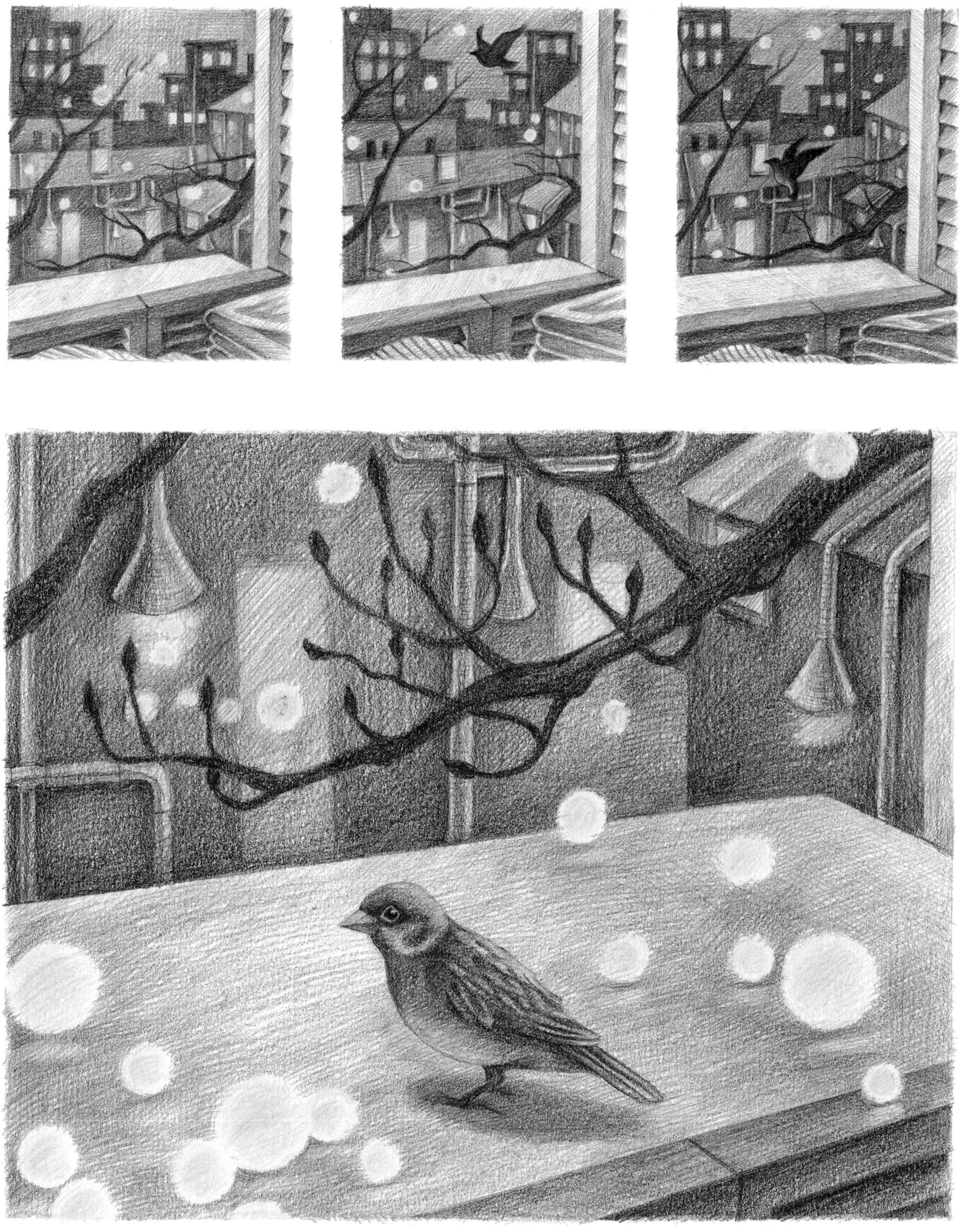

Fantagraphics Books
7563 Lake City Way NE
Seattle, Washington 98115

Editor: Gary Groth
Designer: Jacob Covey
Publicist: Jacquelene Cohen
Associate Publisher: Eric Reynolds
Publisher: Gary Groth

To receive a free full-color catalog of comics, graphic novels, prose novels, artist monographs, and other fine works of artistry, call 1-800-657-1100, or visit www.fantagraphics.com. You may order books at our web site or by phone.

ISBN: 978-1-60699-853-3
Library of Congress Control Number: 2014960291

First Fantagraphics printing: July 2015
Printed in China